A STUDY OF ḤADĪTH:

ʻIlm al-Ḥadīth, Methodology, Literature and Anthology

DR. KHALID MAHMOOD SHAIKH

IQRAʼ International Educational Foundation

Part of a Comprehensive and Systematic Program of Islamic Studies

Junior Level / General

A Study of Hadith

Chief Program Editors
Dr. Abidullah al-Ansari Ghazi
(Ph.D., History of Religion
Harvard University)

Tasneema Khatoon Ghazi
(Ph.D., Curriculum-Reading
University of Minnesota)

Editors & Reviewers
Dr. Gulam H. Aasi
(Ph.D., Temole University)

Maulana Shuaib Qutub
('Alim. Darul-Uloom, Karachi)

Language Editing & Typesetting
Shaista N. Ali
(M. A., Mass Communications,
Karachi University)

Carolyn Baugh
(B.A., Arabic Language & Literature
Duke University)

Mahlaqa Patel
(B.Sc., University of Illinois, Chicago)

Huda Quraishi
(B.Sc.,University of Illinois, Chicago)

Designer
Kathryn Heimberger
(A.A.S., American Academy of Art)

Third Printing May 2007
Printed by Sheridan Books U.S.A

IQRA' International Educational Foundation,
7450 Skokie Blvd., Skokie, IL 60077
Tel: 847-673-4072; Fax: 847-673-4095
E-mail: iqra@aol.com
Website: http://www.iqra.org

Library of Congress Catalog Card Number 96-075423
ISBN # 1-56316-202-4

IQRA's NOTE

To Parents, Teachers and Readers

IQRA' Foundation is pleased to offer for classrooms and the general public Dr. Khalid Mahmood's work entitled *A Study of Ḥadīth: 'Ilm ul-Ḥadīth, Methodology, Literature and Anthology*. This important work on the science of *Ḥadīth* is recommended as an enrichment book or textbook for the students of Islamic Studies on Junior/Senior level. Parents and teachers will find it beneficial to use this book as group reading both at home and in the classroom. A reader will find it most useful as a means of acquiring clarity on important points of Principles and Methodology of *Ḥadīth* and the role of the Prophet ﷺ as the chief interpreter of the Message of Islam.

This publication contains selected samples of *'Aḥādīth* on some important everyday topics relevant to students and general public. Each *Ḥadīth* is produced in Arabic, English transliteration with lucid translation. The author provides information about the narrator and gives full explanation of the *Ḥadīth*.

Dr. Khalid Mahmood is a professor of Islamic Studies at the Islamic University, Islamabad, and Head of the Institute of Islamic Studies at the Azad Jammu and Kashmir University. With his expertise in the field of *Ḥadīth* study, Dr. Mahmood is the ideal person to undertake this venture for IQRA'. The format is easy to read and conducive to classroom teaching. We are confident that any sincere student will greatly benefit from this serious work.

Chief Editors

Jum'ah, 27 Ramadan 1616 Friday, 16 February 1996

CONTENTS

PART I

PART II

Foreword

The Qur'ān is the last revealed Word of God and the basic source of Islamic teachings and laws. *Ḥadīth*, the teachings, sayings and actions of the Rasūlullāh ﷺ, which were accurately reported and collected by his *Sahābah* ﷺ, explain and interpret the teachings of the Qur'ān. The *'Ahadīth* and the *Sunnah* are the second basic sources of Islamic teachings and laws.

I have divided this book into two parts: Part One comprises six chapters which deal with the Science of *Ḥadīth*, and Part Two consists of examples of *Ḥadīth*. The majority of the *'Ahādīth* I have selected deal with social and moral behavior. In Part Two, I have given Arabic text with transliteration, translation, explanation and information about the narrators.

I am grateful that Dr. `Abidullāh Ghāzi, Executive Director, Iqra' Foundation, who asked me to prepare a text book on `Ilm-ul-Ḥadīth for Muslim youth as part of Iqra' Program of Islamic Studies.

I express my heartfelt gratitude to Professor Muhammad Aslam Khan, my close friend and colleague, Mr. `Alī Asghar Chishti, Asst. Professor, for their cooperation and suggestions and Mr. Habib-ur-Rahmān for typing the manuscript. I would request the readers who benefit from the book not to forget me in their prayers.

Khalid Mahmood

ISLAMABAD
12th July, 1995

PART I

CHAPTER I

THE *ḤADĪTH* (اَلحَدِيْثُ): ITS MEANING, CONCEPT AND CLASSIFICATION

The Ḥadīth in its Literal Sense

The Arabic word *Ḥadīth* in its real sense means a tale, speech, chat, conversation or communication. Used as an adjective it means new, modern and recent.

The Ḥadīth in its Technical Sense

In our Islamic Studies class, *Ḥadīth* or Tradition means all the sayings, deeds, decisions of Rasūlullāh, *Ṣalla-(A)llāhu `alai-hi wa-Sallam(a),* his silent approval of the behavior of his *Ṣaḥābah* ﷺ and descriptions of his personality.

The Ḥadīth and The Sunnah

These two words are almost always used to describe the same thing by early scholars as well as present ones, though there is a slight difference in their meanings. *Ḥadīth* really means a story or a report and so represents an account of what happened. The word *Sunnah* means a practice, a way or course, a rule, a mode or manner of life, a precedent, a custom. In its technical sense, it implies the doings and practices of Rasūlullāh ﷺ. The *Sunnah* the actual embodiment of the Will of Allāh ﷻ shown in the actions of Rasūlullāh ﷺ.

With the Muslims, these terms came to be applied to matters relating to Rasūlullāh ﷺ and the customs followed by him and his *Ṣaḥābah*. Records regarding Rasūlullāh's deeds, sayings and his reactions to things said or done in his presence were collected. When the study of these developed, they came to be known under the title *Al-Ḥadīth*. The word *Ḥadīth*, which could be applied to any kind of story, was thus given a new meaning when used in connection with information about Rasūlullāh ﷺ. So in summary, the *Sunnah* is *what was practiced* by Rasūlullāh ﷺ and the *Aḥadīth* are *the records of what was said and practiced* by Rasūlullāh ﷺ.

Parts of Ḥadīth: *Al-'Isnād* (اَلإِسْنَادْ) and *Al-Matn* (اَلْمَتْنْ)

Soon after the death of Rasūlullāh ﷺ the *Ṣaḥābah* had a special concern to safeguard the teachings and practices of Rasūlullāh ﷺ. The life and the teachings of Rasūlullāh ﷺ were fresh in the memory of his *Ṣaḥābah* رضي الله عنهم, so they were not rushing to record everything they remembered. Still, they wanted to make sure that their memory and narration of the *Sunnah* be correct and verifiable. Gradually, a whole system for the preservation of *'Aḥādīth* developed, the like of which the world had never seen. Several works containing collections of *'Aḥādīth* were compiled. Each *Ḥadīth* was prefaced by a chain of narrators called *Al-'Isnād*. *Al-'Isnād* was the chain of people through whom the *Ḥadīth* was transmitted. The second part of the *Ḥadīth* is *Al-Matn*, the content, which reports the teaching or the incident. In this way, the *Ḥadīth* compilers provided not only the information they had received from or about Rasūlullāh ﷺ but also described its authentic source. Every *Ḥadīth* or Tradition must have a chain (*'Isnād*) as well as the Text (*Matn*). For instance, there is a Tradition taken from *Ṣaḥīḥ Al-Bukhāri*, the most authentic work of *Ḥadīth*.

قَالَ ٱلْبُخَارِي أَخْبَرَ سُلَيْمَانُ أَبُو رافِعٍ عَنِ
ٱسْمَاعِيلَ بْنِ جَعْفَرٍ عَنْ نَافِعِ بْنِ مَالِكٍ عَنْ أَبِي
هُرَيْرَةَ قَالَ: قَالَ رَسُولُ ٱللَّهِ صَلَّىٰ ٱللَّهُ
عَلَيْهِ وَسَلَّمَ:" آيَةُ ٱلْمُنَافِقِ ثَلاَثٌ: إِذَا حَدَّثَ كَذَبَ
وَإِذَا وَعَدَ أَخْلَفَ وَإِذَا ٱؤْتُمِنَ خَانَ ".

Al-Bukhārī said that Sulaimān told him saying that 'Ismā`īl b. Jā`far said that Mālik informed him on the authority of his father that 'Abū Hurairah related Rasūlullāh ﷺ saying:
"The signs of a hypocrite are three: whenever he speaks, he tells a lie; whenever he makes a promise, he breaks it; whenever entrusted with something he proves to be dishonest."

In this *Ḥadīth* or Tradition, the chain of narration is: *"Al-Bukhārī said that Sulaimān informed him saying that 'Ismā`īl b. Jā`far said that Mālik informed him on the authority of his father that 'Abū Hurairah related Rasūlullāh (peace be upon him) saying...."*

And the text of the *Ḥadīth* is: *"The signs of a hypocrite are three: whenever he speaks, he tells a lie; whenever he makes a promise, he breaks it; whenever trusted with something, he proves to be dishonest."*

The *Ḥadīth* first contains a series of names and then the actual subject relating to Rasūlullāh ﷺ. The first part is called *'Al-Isnād,* while the actual statement or information relating to Rasūlullāh ﷺ is called *Al-Matn*.

Main Division of The Ḥadīth

The scholars of the *Ḥadīth* literature have divided the Traditions into three categories according to the degree of their reliability. These categories were based on:

(1) The perfection or imperfection of the chain of their transmitters.
(2) The freedom of the texts from any defects.
(3) Acceptance of any *Ḥadīth* by the *Ṣaḥābah* ﷺ, their followers (*At-Tābi`ūn*) and their successors (*At-Tab`bā` at-Tābi`īn*).

1) *Aṣ-Ṣaḥīḥ* (الصَّحِيح) The Authentic Ḥadīth

The True. This name is given to the absolutely correct *Ḥadīth* in which there is no weakness. Both its chain of transmission (*'Al-Isnād*) and the text (*Al-Matn*) are sound, and its text does not contradict any established belief of Islam. Thus, there are four characteristics of *Al-Ḥadīth Aṣ-Ṣaḥīḥ*:

i) Its chain of transmitters is continuous i.e., there is no missing person anywhere in the chain.
ii) Every transmitter possessed the qualities of *`Adl* (righteous conduct) and *Ḍabt* (strong memory).

iii) It should not be an isolated one.
iv) It has no hidden defect.

2) Al-Ḥasan (الحَسَن)
The Good. It is like *Aṣ-Ṣaḥīḥ* Tradition, except for the fact that some of its narrators have been found to have a weaker memory in comparison to the narrators of *Ṣaḥīḥ 'Aḥādīth*.

3) *Aḍ-Ḍa`īf* (الضَعيف)
The Weak. This refers to that Tradition in which there is some problem in either the chain of transmission, in the proper understanding of the transmitter or in its contents, which may be in disagreement with Islamic beliefs and practices.

Aḍ-Ḍa`īf Traditions are further divided according to the degree of problems with their reporters (*ruwāt*) or in the text (*Al-Matn*) of the reports.

A few of these divisions are as follows:

i) ***Al-Mursal*** (المُرْسَل):
A *Ḥadīth* in which a *Tabi`ī* transmits from Rasūlullāh ﷺ directly, dropping the *Ṣaḥābī* from the *'Isnād*.

ii) ***Al-Munqati`*** (المُنْقَطع):
A *Ḥadīth* going back to the *Tabi'ī* only.

iii) ***Al-Mu`dal*** (المُعْضَل):
A *Ḥadīth* in which two continuous narrators are missing in one or more places in the *'Isnād*.

iv) ***Al-Mu`allaq*** (المُعَلَّق):
A *Ḥadīth* in which one or two transmitters are omitted in

the beginning of the *'Isnād*.

'Ahādīth were also divided according to *Al-'Asnād*, the numbers of its narrators:

a) *Al-Mutawātir* (الْمُتَوَاتِر): The Continuous
A *Ḥadīth* reported by a large number of people at different times, that makes it impossible for any falsehood to enter it. This would make agreement upon a lie unthinkable. This condition must be met in the entire chain from its source to its end.

b) *Al-Mashhūr* (أَلْمَشْهُور): Popular
These are the *'Ahādīth* which were originally narrated in the first generation by two to four narrators. Later, on their authority, these were narrated by several narrators.

c) *Al-'Aḥad* (اَلأَحَاد): One Chain of Isnād
A *Ḥadīth* which is narrated in the first three generations by one to four narrators.

***Al-Mawḍū`* (الْمَوْضُوع), The Fabricated**
A false *Ḥadīth* made up by some misguided people. This class of *'Ahādīth* have been carefully uncovered by our learned Islamic scholars in the past. They have no place in true and authentic *'Ahādīth* collections.

* * * * * * * * * * * * * * * *

Exercise:

1. What is the meaning of the word *Ḥadīth*?
2. What is the difference between *Ḥadīth* and *Sunnah*?
3. What are the three main categories of *'Aḥādīth.?*
4. Define *Ḥadīth Ṣaḥīḥ*?
5. What do you understand by the term *Mutawātir*?

CHAPTER 2

SIGNIFICANCE OF THE *'AḤĀDĪTH* IN THE LIGHT OF THE QUR'ĀN

Allāh ﷻ sent His Messengers and Prophets from time to time to guide humankind. This long line of Prophets and Messengers finally ended with the coming of the Last and the Final Prophet, Muhammad ﷺ. He was given the Final Revelation, the Qur'ān for the guidance of humanity for all times to come. He was sent with a complete and perfect Message, Islam. This Divine Guidance for humanity will last until the Day of Judgment.

This Divine Guidance sent through Rasūlullāh ﷺ consists of two parts:

1) The Qur'ān, the Divinely Revealed Book; it is the actual Word of Allāh ﷻ, both its language and in the finality and truthfulness of its message.

2) The *Sunnah* of Rasūlullāh ﷺ or *'Aḥādīth* are his sayings, precepts, teachings and actions which explained the Qur'ān and further completed its message.

The Qur'ān was not revealed to Rasūlullāh ﷺ all at once. It came down gradually over a period of twenty-three years. It was revealed in small portions, as the need arose to help people to understand, memorize and apply its teachings. The role of Rasūlullāh ﷺ, as Allāh's Messenger was to explain, interpret, and actually live its teachings. His life is the Qur'ān in practice.

Rasūlullāh ﷺ not only received the Qur'ān, he was also its most authentic interpreter and teacher. He received from Allāh ﷻ both the words of the Message as well as their meanings. The Qur'ān explains:

﴿ ثُمَّ إِنَّ عَلَيْنَا بَيَانَهُ ﴾ (اَلْقِيَامَةُ ٧٥:١٩)

It is then We Who must explain It (The Qur'ān) and make it clear."
(*Al-Qiyāmah 75:19*)

The role of Rasūlullāh ﷺ was to explain its meanings to others:

﴿وَأَنْزَلْنَا إِلَيْكَ الذِّكْرَ لِتُبَيِّنَ لِلنَّاسِ مَا نُزِّلَ إِلَيْهِمْ وَلَعَلَّهُمْ يَتَفَكَّرُونَ﴾

(اَلنَّحْلُ ١٦:٤٤)

"We revealed to you the Reminder (The Qur'ān), so you may explain to humankind what was sent to them, so that they may meditate and reflect upon it."
(*An-Naḥl 16:44*)

﴿ كَمَآ أَرْسَلْنَا فِيكُمْ رَسُولاً مِّنكُمْ يَتْلُواْ عَلَيْكُمْ

ءَايَـٰتِنَا وَيُزَكِّيكُمْ وَيُعَلِّمُكُمُ ٱلْكِتَـٰبَ وَٱلْحِكْمَةَ

وَيُعَلِّمُكُم مَّا لَمْ تَكُونُواْ تَعْلَمُونَ ﴾

(البقرة ٢:١٥١)

"Just as when We sent a Messenger to you from among yourselves to recite to you Our Signs, purify your lives, and teach you the Book and al-Ḥikmah (the Wisdom) and to teach you what you did not know."
(*Al-Baqarah 2:151*)

The *'Aḥādīth* and the *Sunnah* are also Divinely Inspired and therefore must be followed by Believers. The Qur'ānic description for the *Sunnah* is *al-Ḥikmah,* the Wisdom. The Qur'ān says that Allāh ﷻ ordered Rasūlullāh ﷺ to teach both the Book *(Kitāb)* and the Wisdom *(Ḥikmah)*. Therefore it is now known with the agreement of the *'Ulamā'* that the *'Aḥādīth* are *"the record of the Sunnah"* which is Divinely inspired and guided.

In the Qur'ān, Rasūlullāh ﷺ was given the actual Words of Allah ﷻ; in the *Ḥadīth* the actual words are from Rasūlullāh ﷺ, but the message is still from Allāh ﷻ.

The Qur'ān is very closely associated with the life and teachings of Rasūlullāh ﷺ. He was sent as the best and highest example for us to follow. The Qur'ān says:

﴿ لَّقَدْ كَانَ لَكُمْ فِي رَسُولِ ٱللَّهِ أُسْوَةٌ حَسَنَةٌ ﴾

(اَلأَحْزَابُ ٣٣ : ٢١)

"You have indeed a good example in Allāh's Messenger."
(*Al-'Aḥzāb 33:21*)

His life and teachings are Divinely Inspired:

﴿وَمَا يَنْطِقُ عَنِ ٱلْهَوَىٰٓ إِنْ هُوَ إِلَّا وَحْيٌ يُوحَىٰ ﴾

(اَلنَّجْمُ ٥٣: ٣-٤)

He does not speak from some whim, it is merely inspiration that is revealed (to him).
(*An-Najm 53:3-4*)

He is truly a Messenger sent by Allāh ﷻ and obedience to him is required by all Muslims. The Qur'ān says:

﴿ قُلْ أَطِيعُواْ ٱللَّهَ وَأَطِيعُواْ ٱلرَّسُولَ ... ﴾

(اَلنُّورُ ٢٤ : ٥٤)

"Say: Obey Allāh, and obey the Messenger..."
(*An-Nūr 24:54*)

The verses quoted above define the role of Rasūlullāh ﷺ as guide, teacher, and leader.

The Qur'ān is a complete code of life only when it is followed in the light of the *Sunnah* of Rasūlullāh ﷺ. The fundamentals and principles of Islam are laid down in the Qur'ān, but they are explained and elaborated in the *Sunnah* and *'Aḥādīth*. The Qur'ān speaks about many issues and orders many obligations, but leaves the details for the *'Aḥādīth* to explain. For example, the orders for *Ṣalāh*, *Ṣawm*, *Zakāh*, and *Ḥajj* are found in the Qur'ān; the details of their performance were taught by Rasūlullāh ﷺ and are preserved in the *'Aḥādīth*. One cannot perform any Islamic obligation without the guidance of both the Qur'ān and the *Sunnah*.

* * * * * * * * * * * * * * *

Exercise:

1. Briefly describe the importance of *'Aḥādīth* in relation to the Qur'ān.

2. In *Sūrah al-Baqarah* (2:151) the role of Rasūlullāh ﷺ is to teach 'the Book and the Wisdom.' What do you understand by 'the Wisdom' and what is the relationship between Qur'ān and 'the Wisdom'?

CHAPTER 3

THE AUTHENTICITY OF THE *'AḤĀDĪTH*
(The Collection, Preservation and Compilation)

Before we discuss the collection and preservation of the *'Aḥādīth*, we must briefly study the steps taken by Rasūlullāh ﷺ himself for the teaching of his *Sunnah* to his *Ṣaḥābah* ؓ and also to those who were not present with him. Before migrating to Madīnah, Rasūlullāh ﷺ sent two of his *Ṣaḥābah* ؓ to teach the new Muslims of Madīnah. In this way, the people of Madīnah learned the Qur'ān and the *Sunnah* of Rasūlullāh ﷺ.

Immediately upon his arrival to Madīnah, Rasūlullāh ﷺ built *Masjid an-Nabī*, the Prophet's Mosque, and built his living quarters next to it. Many *Ṣaḥābah* ؓ lived in the *Masjid* on the *Ṣuffah*, which is a type of elevated platform. Here, they learned the meaning of the Qur'ān from Rasūlullāh ﷺ and studied his *Sunnah*. Thus, the *Ṣuffah* was actually the first Islamic University. It is not surprising that most of the *'Aḥādīth* are related through the *'Aṣḥāb as-Ṣuffah* (the People of the Platform). There were nine other *Masājid* in the city of Madīnah, and almost all of them were used as Islamic schools as well. In *Masjid an-Nabī*, Rasūlullāh ﷺ himself was the teacher and guide. He taught and advised his *Ṣaḥābah* ؓ:

"Pass on knowledge from me, even if it be only one sentence."

The same message is found in his Farewell *Khuṭbah*, where Rasūlullāh ﷺ said, *"Learn from me the rules of Islam, for I may not be with you next year."* Then he told his *Ṣaḥābah* رضي الله عنهم:

"Those who are present (here) should convey the Message to those who are absent."

Rasūlullāh ﷺ advised his *Ṣaḥābah* رضي الله عنهم:

" صَلُّوا كَمَا رَأَيْتُمُونِي أُصَلِّي ".

"Pray as you see me praying."

We know from history and the life stories of the *Ṣaḥābah* that it was a common practice among them to learn from Rasūlullāh ﷺ and to teach others about his deeds and sayings. Many groups of people came to Madīnah to accept Islam and learn about the teachings of the Qur'ān and *Sunnah*. Then, they were asked to teach their own people what they had learned. On many occasions Rasūlullāh ﷺ sent his *Ṣaḥābah* رضي الله عنهم to teach Islam to the newly converted Arab tribes.

Islam places great importance on the learning and teaching of religion. Rasūlullāh ﷺ stated:

"Whenever Allāh intends to do good for someone, He gives him the knowledge and understanding of His religion."
(*Al-Bukhārī* and *Muslim*)

Rasūlullāh ﷺ further said:

"When a man dies, his acts come to an end, except for three things:
as-Ṣadaqah al-Jāriyah (recurring charity); knowledge from which benefit continues to be reaped, and the prayers of a good offspring for his or her parents."

So far, we have discussed the way Rasūlullāh ﷺ taught the Qur'ān and his *Sunnah* to the Muslim community and the steps he took to spread it. Now, we shall discuss the methods adopted by the *Ṣaḥābah* to learn and preserve the knowledge they received from Rasūlullāh ﷺ. The *Ṣaḥābah* had three methods of learning:

1. **Memorization**
2. **Recording**
3. **Practice**

1. Memorization

In the early Muslim society, everyone's major goal was to learn Islam directly from Rasūlullāh ﷺ. Most Arabs of that time had excellent memories and they were known to learn by heart many verses of their poets and their tribal histories. Similarly, the *Ṣaḥābah* always tried to observe the actions of Rasūlullāh ﷺ, remember his sayings and follow them in their everyday lives. By doing so, they developed a close connection to Rasūlullāh ﷺ, no matter how distant in space or time he was.

Rasūlullāh ﷺ had a unique method of teaching: to make memorizing and understanding easy, Rasūlullāh ﷺ would repeat important things three times. He would then listen as his followers repeated what he had told them to be sure that they understood. As it was not possible for all of the hundreds and hundreds of *Ṣaḥābah* ﷺ to attend the *Majlis* (study circle) of Rasūlullāh ﷺ on every occasion, those who were present taught those who were absent. This practice did not, however, end with the *Ṣaḥābah* ﷺ but has continued ever since. In the *Sīrah* literature, we find a large number of the *Ṣaḥābah* ﷺ advising their successors to memorize *'Aḥādīth* either in groups or individually.

2. Recording

In the beginning, the *'Aḥādīth* were not written but were memorized because the *Ṣaḥābah* ﷺ feared that people would confuse the *Ḥadīth* with the Qur'ān. However, when the written text of the Qur'ān became widespread, many *Ṣaḥābah* started taking notes on *'Aḥādīth*. We know the names of many *Ṣaḥābah* ﷺ who used to write down *'Aḥādīth* during the life of Rasūlullāh ﷺ. In several instances, Rasūlullāh ﷺ himself dictated to them.

There are many other recorded documents that were written at the insistence of Rasūlullāh ﷺ. All the letters of Rasūlullāh ﷺ to kings, rulers, and chieftains, orders and instructions to Muslim officials and governors are all in the category of written *Sunnah*. Some of those letters are very lengthy and contain legal matters about *Zakāh*, taxation, forms of worship etc. There are about sixty-five other documents which originate from Rasūlullāh ﷺ.

The number of these documents, however, is smaller than those written down by later scholars. Not all the *Ṣaḥābah* ﷺ transmitted equal numbers of *'Aḥādīth*. Some of them dedicated their lives to learning and teaching the *'Aḥādīth*, while others were engaged in other duties. Few of them transmitted more than a thousand *'Aḥādīth*. In reality, most of them transmitted fewer than that.

The names of those *Ṣaḥābah* ﷺ who transmitted *'Aḥādīth* in large numbers are as follows:

1). 'Abū Hurairah ﷺ. It is commonly known that 'Abū Hūrairah transmitted 5,374 *'Aḥādīth*. Actually, this is the number of channels through which *'Aḥādīth* were transmitted by him. The most recent research shows that the number of *'Aḥādīth* transmitted by him is only 1,236. He is reported to have had actual books of *Ḥadīth* in his possession. At least nine of his students recorded *'Aḥādīth* from him.

2). 'Ibn `Umar ﷺ transmitted 2,630 *'Aḥādīth*. We have authentic reports that he had a written collection of *'Aḥādīth*. At least eight of his students wrote *'Aḥādīth* collections from him.

3). 'Anas 'Ibn Mālik ﷺ, who had served Rasūlullāh ﷺ for ten years transmitted 2,286 *'Aḥādīth*. At least sixteen persons recorded *'Aḥādīth* from him in written form.

4). *'Umm al-Mu'minīn* `Ā'ishah ﷺ transmitted 2,210 *'Aḥādīth*. At least three persons had *'Aḥādīth* from her in written form including her nephew, `Urwah, one of the greatest scholars among the *At-Tabi`ūn.*

5). 'Ibn `Abbas ﷺ transmitted 1,660 *'Aḥādīth*. At least nine of his students had *'Aḥādīth* from him in written form.

6). 'Abū Sa`īd al-Khudrī ﷺ transmitted 1,170 *'Aḥādīth*.

Those *Ṣaḥābah* who are recorded as transmitting less than one thousand *'Aḥādīth* are listed as follows:

1). 'Ibn Mas`ūd ﷺ transmitted 748 *'Aḥādīth*. We have no information about his students who wrote down *'Aḥādīth* from him but his own book was in the possession of his son.

2). `Abdullāh 'Ibn `Amr 'Ibn Al-`Ās ﷺ transmitted 700 *'Aḥādīth*. We learn that he used to write down *'Aḥādīth* while Rasūlullāh ﷺ was alive and titled his book by the name of *Al-Ṣaḥīfah aṣ-Ṣādiqah*. At least seven of his students had *'Aḥādīth* from him in written form.

3). `Umar 'Ibn al-Khattab ﷺ, the second *Khalīfah*, transmitted 537 *'Aḥādīth*. He used to quote *'Aḥādīth* in official letters and in this way, many Traditions are recorded by him.

4). `Alī 'Ibn 'Abī Tālib ﷺ, the fourth *Khalīfah* transmitted 536 Traditions. At least eight of his students had his *'Aḥādīth* in the written form.

5). 'Abū Mūsa Al-'Ash`ārī ﷺ transmitted 360 *'Aḥādīth*. Some of his Traditions were in the possession of 'Ibn `Abbās ﷺ in the written form.

6). 'Al-Barā' Ibn `Āzīb ﷺ transmitted 305 *'Aḥādīth*. He used to dictate *'Aḥādīth*.

In light of the facts mentioned above, it is quite safe to assume that most of the *'Aḥādīth* of Rasūlullāh ﷺ were written down during the lifetimes of the *Sahābah* ﷺ. Now it is an established fact that the *Ṣaḥābah* ﷺ, *At-Tabi`ūn*, and later scholars not only memorized the *'Aḥādīth* of the Prophet ﷺ but also recorded them in books and manuals.

3. Practical Demonstration

Learning by practice is the most effective way to acquire any kind of knowledge. If we go through the *Ḥadīth* literature, we find that a great many *'Aḥādīth* pertain to our practical life. The knowledge of religion is something to be practiced and not simply discussed. The *Ṣaḥābah* ﷺ learned by observing the ways of Rasūlullāh ﷺ and then applying what they saw to their own practices.

`Umar رضي الله عنه, the second *Khalīfah*, gave his governors the duty of teaching the Qur'ān and the *Sunnah* of Rasūlullāh ﷺ. He used to send teachers out for this purpose. Whenever they had the opportunity or felt the need, those *Ṣaḥābah* رضي الله عنهم who had the knowledge of the *Hadīth* of Rasūlullāh ﷺ took part in teaching it to others.

After the death of Rasūlullāh ﷺ, his *Sahābah* رضي الله عنهم took up his mission. A quarter of a century after his death, Islam spread to most of the lands of the Middle East. The *Ṣaḥābah* رضي الله عنهم of Rasūlullāh ﷺ were pioneers in the spreading of Islam and the knowledge of the *Sunnah* of Rasūlullāh ﷺ went with those *Ṣaḥābah* رضي الله عنهم to the new Muslim lands.

Before the *Ṣaḥābah* رضي الله عنهم died, they passed the torch of knowledge of the Qur'ān and the *Ḥadīth* to the next generation, who had to learn and be prepared to accept this great responsibility. Thus, we find that in the first century of the *Hijrah,* hundreds of booklets of *Ḥadīth* were in circulation. In the next century, the knowledge of *Ḥadīth* was so widespread that it is not possible to count the books and manuals which were in circulation during that period.

Thus, the *'Ummah* of Muhammad ﷺ has responded to his advice, "Teach from me even if it be one sentence," and preserved and spread his message throughout the world.

* * * * * * * * * * * * * * * *

Exercise:

1. What steps were undertaken by Rasūlullāh ﷺ for the spread of Islamic knowledge after he arrived in Madinah?

2. How was the *Sunnah* preserved by the *Ṣaḥābah* ؓ of Rasūlullāh ﷺ?

3. Who transmitted the largest number of *'Aḥādīth* from Rasūlullāh ﷺ?

4. Did the *Ṣaḥābah* ؓ or the *At-Tabi'ūn* possess any books or manuals on *Ḥadīth?*

5. It is sometimes believed that the *'Aḥādīth* were transmitted orally for at least one hundred years, and after that time the scholar Az-Zuhrī recorded them by the order of the Umayyad *Khalīfah,* `Umar 'Ibn `Abd al-`Azīz. Do you agree with this? If not, give examples to support of your answer.

CHAPTER 4

KINDS OF *'AḤADĪTH* COLLECTIONS

In the first century of the *Hijrah,* several hundred books of varying sizes dealing with *'Aḥādīth* were in circulation. These books which appeared in the first or early second century of *Hijrah,* contained the *'Aḥādīth* of Rasūlullāh ﷺ only. These were simply collections without any arrangement of the material. The books containing *'Aḥādīth* of Rasūlullāh ﷺ were mixed with legal decisions of the Rightly-Guided Caliphs, other *Ṣaḥābah* and *At-Tābi`ūn*.

In the second century of *Hijrah,* the trend changed somewhat and books covering almost all aspects legal issues began to appear. The book of Imām Mālik called *Al-Muwatta'* belongs to this period. It was arranged according to chapters, and covered the whole range of human life, from *`Ibādāt (Ṣalāh, Ṣawm, Zakāh, Ḥajj),* to social, agricultural and economic issues.

At the end of the second century, books containing only the *'Aḥādīth* of Rasūlullāh ﷺ with a certain organized arrangement began to appear. Later on, in the third and fourth centuries most of the books on *'Aḥādith* which appeared contained only the words of Rasūlullāh ﷺ. Some books which appeared in this period were compiled on the pattern of the second century, such as *Musannaf* of `Abd-ur-Razzāq and 'Ibn 'Abī Shaibah or *Al-'Awṣaṭ* of 'Ibn Al-Mundhir. *Ḥadīth* books were compiled on different patterns and were named *Musnad Jām`ī, Sunan, Mustakhraj* or *Mu`jam.* Some of these collections are divided into categories as follows:

1. Al-Jām`ī` (اَلْجَامِع)

A book containing all kinds of *'Aḥādīth* is called *Jām`ī*, that is, it contains *'Aḥādīth* concerning *Siyar* (plural of *Sīrah*, biography of Rasūlullāh ﷺ, *'Ādāb* (social behavior), *Tafsīr* (exegesis of the Qur'ān), *`Aqīdah* (Belief), *Fitnah* (temptation, discord, civil war, trial), *'Aḥkām* (laws of all kinds), *Al-'Ishārāt* (signs of the Last Day), and *Manāqib* (fine qualities of Rasūlullāh ﷺ, his *Ṣaḥābah* رضي الله عنهم, his tribe etc.). The Bukhārī book is therefore *Jām`ī* as it contains *'Aḥādīth* on all these chapters.

2. Al-Musnad (اَلْمُسْنَد)

Musnad is a kind of collection in which *'Aḥādīth* are arranged according to the names of the *Ṣaḥābah* رضي الله عنهم. Some of them begin with the four *Khulafā' ar-Rashidūn* رضي الله عنهم, followed by the remaining six of them who had the tidings of Paradise from Rasūlullāh ﷺ, followed by the *Ṣaḥābah* رضي الله عنهم who embraced Islam first and so on. Some of the books are arranged by region and some alphabetically, for example, the *Musnad of Aḥmad b. Ḥanbal*.

3. As-Sunan (اَلسُّنَن)

In this collection, *'Aḥādīth* were recorded according to their subject and the subject matter arranged under the headings of law books. Such collections were previously called *'Abwāb* and *Muṣannafāt*. For example *Sunan 'Ibn Mājah and Sunan Nasā'ī*.

4. Al-Mu`jam (اَلْمُعْجَم)

These differ from one author to another. Sometimes it is arranged according to alphabetical listing of names of the

Sahābah ﷺ, other times according to region, and some other times according to the alphabetical listing of the names of the teachers of the compilers, as has been done by Imām Aṭ-Ṭabarānī in his *Al-Mu`jam Aṣ-Ṣaghīr*.

5. Al-Mustakhraj (الْمُسْتَخْرَج)

Al-Mustakhrāj, a later scholar, chooses one of the early works like *Ṣaḥīḥ Al-Bukhārī*, and narrates the same *Ḥadīth* in his books, passing Bukhārī, joining *'Isnād* of Bukhārī in upper part, with the teachers of Al-Bukhārī. There are many books written in this pattern by later scholars i.e., *Al-Mustakhraj* of 'Ismā`īl on Al-Bukhārī.

6. Al-Mustadrak (اَلْمُسْتَدْرَك)

In this collection of *'Aḥādīth*, the author has included in his book the Traditions which were missed by other compilers, even though the transmitters fulfilled the conditions laid down by the authors for the acceptance of *Ḥadīth*. For example, Al-Bukhārī and Muslim laid down strict conditions for acceptance of *Ḥadīth* for their *Ṣaḥīḥain* collections. Only if all the conditions laid down were fulfilled by the narrators, was the *Ḥadīth* accepted; otherwise it was rejected. Later on, the scholar Al-'Ahkām studied and discovered more *'Aḥādith* that both Bukhārī and Muslim had left out, but in which the narrators did fulfill the required conditions. Imām Al-'Ahkām included these types of *'Aḥādīth* in his book, *Al-Mustadrak*.

* * * * * * * * * * * * * * * *

Exercise:

1. "The books and manuals of *'Aḥādīth* which appeared in the first century of *Hijrah* were only collections, without any organized arrangement of the material." Do you agree with this statement? If so, give reasons to support your answer.

2. Write short paragraphs on each of the following:

   a) *Musnad*

   b) *Mu'jam*

3. What is the difference between *Jām'ī* and *Sunan*?

CHAPTER 5

CRITICISM OF THE *'AḤĀDĪTH*

The *Ṣaḥābah* ﷺ, their successors (*at-Tabi'ūn*) and later scholars took extreme care to memorize the Traditions of Rasūlullāh ﷺ, write them down and teach them. No other people were known to have been so careful in preserving the teachings of their prophets and teachers. In fact, in most cases, later generations added many untrue beliefs into their Prophets' lives and teachings.

The Muslims were warned by Rasūlullāh ﷺ who said, "Anyone who tells a lie about me, will find his place in the Hell-Fire." He also ordered Muslims to truthfully tell others about his sayings and actions. The Qur'ān itself has spoken in detail about him, describing his personality , his message, and his teachings very clearly. Thus, every truth spoken in his name must be judged against the teachings of the Qur'ān.

Early Muslim scholars were quite aware of these problems and they developed a thorough system of examination and criticism to test the authenticity of each *Ḥadīth*. These principles for examining the authenticity of the *'Aḥādīth* were quite unique to the ancient world and have no parallel in present scholarship. These rules cover both parts of the *Ḥadīth*: the *'Isnād* (chain of transmission) and the *Matn* (the text).

In their attempt to set up tests of authenticity which would exclude false material, the *Muḥaddithūn* established a method in which the *'Isnād*, the chain of narrators, and the *Matn,* the basic text, were carefully examined. An elaborate system was created to verify the personality and trustworthiness of each narrator in the chain. The *Muḥaddithūn* developed a system of historical biographies of the narrators of the *'Aḥādīth* to check their backgrounds and characters. On the basis of the authenticity of *'Isnād*, *'Aḥādīth* were established as excellent, good, fair, weak, etc.

To a Muslim, the *'Isnād* is just as important an element in a *Ḥadīth* as is the *Matn* (the content). Since the *Ḥadīth* consists of two parts, principles of *Ḥadīth* criticism are based upon both the *'Isnād* and the *Matn.*

The following is a summary of the rules and principles of *'Isnād* criticism:

1. All the *'Aḥādīth* must be traceable to the original reporter through a chain of narrators.

2. In addition to having a good memory, these narrators must be truthful, of excellent character, and have high qualities of mind and heart.

3. Every *Ḥadīth* which reported an event or a happening that occurred frequently in the presence of a large number of people must have been originally reported by several narrators.

As far as the *Matn* is concerned, some of the following rules were laid down:

1. The *Hadīth* should not contradict the text of the Qur'ān, the teachings of the Qur'ān and the accepted basic principles of Islam.

2. The *Hadīth* should not contradict the Traditions already deemed reliable and authentic by the authorities under these rules.

3. The *Hadīth* which sings the praises and excellence of any tribe, place or persons should sometimes be closely examined.

4. The *Hadīth* that contains some remarks of Rasūlullāh ﷺ which are not in keeping with the Islamic belief and the position of Rasūlullāh ﷺ or such expressions as may not be befitting his honor.

Early Muslims understood that the importance of the *Hadīth* is second only to that of the Qur'ān. Knowing this, they developed many rules for checking the *'Ahadīth*. Thanks to this effort, thousands of the sayings of Rasūlullāh ﷺ have been preserved for us today.

* * * * * * * * * * * * * * *

Exercise:

1. What are false *'Ahādīth*? What did Rasūlullāh ﷺ say about them?

2. What were some of the steps taken by early Muslim scholars to keep *'Ahādīth* free from any problems?

3. What where some of the rules that the great scholars of Islam set up to differentiate between the genuine *'Ahādīth* and the fake ones?

CHAPTER 6

MAJOR WORKS OF *'AHĀDĪTH* AND THEIR COMPILERS

As explained in the previous chapter, the recording of the Traditions of Rasūlullāh ﷺ started in his lifetime. In the early years, books contained only the narration of Rasūlullāh ﷺ. After the death of Rasūlullāh ﷺ, even the decisions of the *Sahābah* ﷺ were recorded as *Aḥādīth*. By the middle of the first century *Hijrah*, the books and manuals recording the *Ahādīth* began to appear. Due to the enthusiasm with which Muslims recorded the sayings and actions of Rasūlullāh ﷺ, the number of these books continued to increase. They numbered over two thousand by the second century *Hijrah*. In the third century *Hijrah*, *Aḥadīth* literature became very widespread. In this period *Fuqahā'*, Islamic jurists, started compiling the *Fiqh* in the light of the Qur'ān and the *Sunnah*. With the development of *Hadīth* rules of classification, more attempts were made to compile authentic collections. Even today, we have over one hundred books of *Ahādīth* but not all of them carry the same weight. Some are regarded as more authentic and are commonly used. We will list some of these here:

1. *The Muwatta' of Imām Mālik*

The compiler of this work was Mālik (93-179 A.H.) b. 'Anas b. Mālik. He was born in 93 A.H. in the city of Madīnah. His grandfather, Mālik, was a *Tabi'ī*, and his great-grandfather was a *Sahābī* of Rasūlullāh ﷺ. Living in the center of Islamic scholarship, he did not travel to study

'Ahādīth, and he had many good opportunities to learn from the famous scholars of the Islamic world who came to visit Madīnah. The number of his students exceeded one thousand. He is also the author of many books on the subject. Imām Mālik reached the level of *Mujtahid*, and is the founder of one of the Four *Madhāhib* of the *Ahla (a)s-Sunnah wa (a)l-Jamā'ah*.

The *Muwātta'* is not purely a book of *Ahādīth*. It contains the *'Ahādīth* of Rasūlullāh ☙, and legal opinions of the *Sahābah* ☙, the Successors and of some later authorities. In this work, he collected a huge amount of material, applied the *Hadīth* methodology and selected a few thousand *'Ahādīth* from it. Whatever knowledge that Mālik aquired in the space of forty years is available in *Muwātta'*. A vast amount of literature has been produced on this book; perhaps it stands next to the *Sahīh of Al-Bukhārī* in importance.

2. *The Musnad of Imām 'Ahmad*

The author of the *Musnad*, 'Imām 'Ahmad 'ibn Hanbal (164-246 AH), began to study *'Ahādīth* in 179 A.H. He memorized several hundred thousand *'Ahādīth* in his lifetime. He is one of the leading personalities in Islamic history who combined knowledge of *'Ahādīth* and Law. He wrote many works, some of which have been published and a few of which are lost. The *Musnad* is the most famous of all his works. It was published in six volumes in 1313 A.H. A number of books have been written about the *Musnad* of Imām Ahmad. Like Imām Mālik, he also reached the level of *Mujtahid* and is the founder of one of the Four *Madhāhib* of the four schools of the *Ahlu (a) s-Sunnah wa (a)l- Jamā'ah*.

However, until now, the number of *'Ahādīth* in the *Musnad* have not been counted. Scholars estimate that there are between 30,000 to 40,000 *'Ahādīth*. This is perhaps the largest book on *Hadīth* in the Muslim world.

3. *Sahīh Al-Bukhārī*

The author 'Abū `Abdullāh Muhammad b. 'Ismā`īl (194-256 A.H.) was from the city of Bukhārā, which is now in modern-day Uzbekistan. His father, Ismā`īl, was a scholar of *Ahādīth*. Al-Bukhārī began the study of *Ahādīth* when he was less than ten years old. By the age of sixteen, he had memorized many books of the famous early scholars. Unsatisfied with just the memorization of the *Ahādīth*, he also studied the biographies of the narrators. He could produce by memory the dates of birth and death and other important biographical information of the narrator.

Al-Bukhārī's reputation spread far and wide, because of his authority on the subject and his valuable work on *Hadīth*. He compiled many books, but his most famous is *Al-Jām`ī Al-Bukhārī* (known universally as *As-Sahīh Al-Bukhārī*, or *As-Sahīh*). In the compilation of this work he displayed a great critical ability and the most scrupulous accuracy. He established the rule that the transmitters must stand in a continuous and unbroken chain, meaning they must have lived during the life of the other and must actually have met.

Al-Bukhārī put *Ahādith* into chapters which covered a whole range of *Fiqh* (Islamic Jurisprudence). His work is divided into ninety-seven books (or chapters), which are further divided into 3,450 chapters. The number of *'Aḥādīth* in his book is 9,082. However, many of them were repeated with different *'Isnād*. Without repetition, the number goes down to 2,602. Hundreds of explanations have been written on the book over the centuries. *As-Sahīh* is regarded as the most authentic book after the Qur'ān.

4. *Sahīh Muslim*:

'Abu-(a)l-Husain b. Al-Hajjāj b. Muslim (204-264), began his study of *Aḥādīth* at the age of 15. He traveled widely to collect *'Aḥādīth* and went to Arabia, Egypt and Iraq, where he found great opportunities to listen to famous learned scholars. He was a remarkable writer and also wrote many books on *Fiqh* (Islamic Law) and biographies but, unfortunately, these are lost.

The book for which he is best known is the *Sahīh Muslim*. Out of 300,000 Traditions collected by him, only those which are recognized as absolutely *Sahīh* were selected by him. He established the practice that the narrators must stand in unbroken successions; they must have lived at the same time and there must have been a possibility of their actual contact. He paid so much attention to the *'Isnād* that a Tradition is often followed by several different *'Isnād*. The *Sahīh* is introduced by a very useful discussion on the science of *Ḥadīth* itself and many other important topics of Islamic Law. *Sahīh Muslim* is recognized as being second only to *Sahīh Al-Bukhārī*. These two collections, *Sahīh Al-Bukharī* and *Sahīh Muslim,* are collectively called *As-Sahihain,* the Two Most Authentic Collections. If the two of them reported a *Hadīth*, it has the highest level of credibility and it is called *Muttafaqun `Alaihi (*One Agreed Upon). Many commentaries are written on *"As-Sahihain"* and these have been part of lessons in Islamic Studies in Islamic institutions for centuries.[1]

5. *Sunan At-Tirmidhī*

'Imām At-Tirmidhī (209-279 A.H.) traveled widely in Iran, Irāq and the Hijāz to collect the Traditions. He was very much influenced by 'Imām Al-Bukhārī. He wrote many books, but his most famous work is *'Al-Jām`ī`* or *Sunan At-Tirmidhī.* He discussed the legal opinions of early Imāms regarding the subject of *'Ahadith.* While discussing the quality of the *'Ahādīth,* he points out the *`illah* (weakness or defect), if there is any. The work is divided into 50 chapters *(Kutub).* Altogether, it contains 3,956 *'Ahādīth.*

6. *Sunan 'Abū Dāwūd*

Imām 'Abū Dāwūd (202-275 A.H.) was a trusted narrator of *'Ahādīth* and a careful collector and compiler. He was also a well-known *Faqīh.* 'Abū Dāwūd said that he collected half a million *'Ahādīth* out of which he selected 4,800 absolutely authentic *'Ahadith.* In his *Sunan 'Abū Dāwūd*, he adopted the method of arranging *'Ahādīth* by different topics.

7. *Sunan An-Nasā'ī*

Imām An-Nasā'ī (210-303 A.H.) took long journeys to learn Traditions of Rasūlullāh ﷺ. He started his study of *Hadīth* at the age of fifteen, when he began extensive travels

---

[1] For some of the books of *Ahādīth* and anthologies, English translations are available.

to far off places to collect *'Ahādīth*. He is known to have visited parts of Iran, Irāq, Arabia, Syria, Egypt and Al-Jazīrah.

8. *Sunan of 'Ibn Mājah*

'Ibn Mājah (209-273 AH) also traveled extensively to collect the Traditions of Rasūlullāh ﷺ. The scholars of Islam unanimously agree about 'Ibn Mājah's great knowledge and trustworthiness. His *Sunan* contains 4,341 *'Aḥādīth*. It has very little repetition and it is one of the best in arrangement of chapters.

Later developments in the arrangement of collections took place about the middle of the third century when *'Ahādīth* were the guidance for the practice and beliefs of the community. Gradually, these six collections which were compiled in the latter part of the third century of *Hijrah,* succeeded in gaining such popular approval that later generations accepted them as the six most reliable collections. These became known as *As-Sihāh As-Sittah (The Six Authentic Books on Ḥadīth)*. They are as follows:

1. *Sahīh Al-Bukhārī*
2. *Sahīh Muslim*
3. *Jām`ī-At-Tirmidhī*
4. *Sunan Nasā'ī*
5. *Sunan 'Abū Dāwūd*
6. *Sunan 'Ibn Mājah*

* * * * * * * * * * * * * * *

Exercise:

1. Who are the authors of the *Muwatta'* and the *Musnad*? Briefly describe the main characteristics of both collections of *'Ahādīth*.

2. Explain Al-Bukhārī's method of arranging the *'Ahādīth*.

3. Write a brief paragraph on each of the following:

   i) *Sunan Nasā'ī*
   ii) *Sunan 'Ibn Mājah*
   iii) *Sunan 'Abū Dāwūd*.

PART II

The 'Aḥādīth

CHAPTER 7

THE IMPORTANCE OF INTENTION

عَنْ عُمَرَ بْنِ ٱلخَطَّابِ رَضِيَ ٱللَّهُ عَنْهُ قَالَ: سَمِعْتُ رَسُولَ ٱللَّهِ
صَلَّىٰ ٱللَّهُ عَلَيهِ وَسَلَّمَ يَقُولُ: " إِنَّمَا ٱلأَعْمَالُ بِٱلنِّيَّاتِ وإِنَّمَا لِكُلِّ
ٱمْرِىءٍ مَا نَوَىٰ، فَمَنْ كَانَتْ هِجْرَتُهُ إِلَى ٱللَّهِ وَرَسُولِهِ
فَهِجْرَتُهُ إِلَى ٱللَّهِ وَرَسُولِهِ وَمَنْ كَانَتْ هِجْرَتُهُ لِدُنْيَا
يُصِيبُهَا أَوِ ٱمْرَأَةٍ يَنْكِحُهَا فَهِجْرَتُهُ
إِلَىٰ مَا هَاجَرَ إِلَيْهِ".
(رَوَاهُ ٱلبُخَارِي وَمُسْلِمٌ)

Transliteration

`An `Umar 'Ibn Al-Khattābi Radiya-(A)llāhu `an-hu, qāla:

Sami`tu Rasūla-(A)llāhi Salla-(A)llāhu `alai-hi wa-Sallam yaqūlu: "Innama-(a)l'a`mālu bi-(a)l-niyyāti wa-'innamā li-kulli 'imri'in mā nawā, fa-man kānat hijratu-hu 'il(a)-Allāhi wa-Rasūli-hi fa-hijratu-hu 'il(a)-Allāhi wa-Rasūli-hi wa-man kānat hijratu-hu 'li(a)d-dunyā yusību-hā 'aw 'imra'atin yankihu-hā fa-hijratu-hu 'ilā mā hājara 'ilai-hi."
(Al-Bukhāri wa-Muslim)

Translation

`Umar 'Ibn Al-Khaṭṭāb ﷺ said that he heard the Messenger of Allāh ﷺ saying: "Actions are determined by intention, and every man shall have that which he intended. So, he whose migration was for Allāh and His Messenger, his migration was for Allāh and His Messenger, and he whose migration was to get some worldly benefit or to take some woman in marriage, his migration was for that which he migrated for."

(*Narrated by Bukhārī and Muslim*)

A. About the Reporter

`Umar 'Ibn Al-Khaṭṭāb ﷺ was the second of our *Khulafā' ar-Rāshidah*. He embraced Islam before Rasūlullāh ﷺ migrated to Madīnah. He transmitted 537 *'Aḥādīth*. He used to quote *'Aḥādīth* in official letters and, in this way, many *'Aḥādīth* were recorded from him.

B. Explanation of the Text (*Matn*)

In this *Ḥadīth*, it is described that every human action is based upon its intention. In other words, a deed will be deemed good and carry weight in the Sight of Allāh ﷻ only if it is done with the intention to please only Allāh ﷻ. Allāh ﷻ judges the worth and value of an action by the motive with which it is done.

It should not, however, be imagined that even evil and *Ḥarām* deeds that are committed with a good intention become virtuous and deserve Divine reward. The deeds that are wicked in themselves and have been condemned by Allāh ﷻ and His Messenger ﷺ will remain hateful in the Sight of Allāh ﷻ and deserving of Divine Punishment.

This *Ḥadīth* tells us that even good actions will stop being praiseworthy if one does them with the wrong intention or just to show off. For example, a person might offer the *Salāh* just to impress others with his devotion to Allāh سبحانه وتعالى. According to this *Ḥadīth*, this will earn him nothing in the Judgement of Allāh سبحانه وتعالى.

To make *Hijrah* for the sake of Allah سبحانه وتعالى is a very important concept in Islam. If a person migrates from the land of non-believers to the land of the believers and endures all the hardships, but his migration has some worldly motive behind it, such as marrying a woman who lives in that country, then his migration will not entitle him to receive Divine reward.

Another *Ḥadīth* describes three persons who fulfilled their religious responsibilities completely, but their intentions were not pure. Because of their intentions, they were condemned to Hell by Allāh سبحانه وتعالى.

The first person in this *Ḥadīth* to be called to account will be a *Shahīd*, a Martyr, killed in *Jihād*. When he is presented, Allāh سبحانه وتعالى will remind him of His Blessings, which he will recall without hesitation. Allāh سبحانه وتعالى will then say to him: "Tell Me what have you done for Me?"

He will reply: "I made *Jihād* in Your Way, and even laid down my life in seeking Your good pleasure." *"You are a liar"* Allāh سبحانه وتعالى will remark. "You made *Jihād* simply because you wanted people to say such a one was a valiant fighter; and it has been said already." He will, thereupon, be thrown headlong into the fire of Hell.

In the same way, an *`Ālim* who learned the whole Qur'ān and then taught it to others will be brought before Allāh سبحانه وتعالى. The Lord will ask him, "What did you do for Me?" He will say, "I learned Your Book and studied Your religion myself and taught it to others, and I did it all for Your sake alone." "You are a liar!" Allāh سبحانه وتعالى will say. "You desired only that people should say that such a one was a great scholar and a reciter of the Qur'ān and that has been said already." The person will, therefore, be cast into Hell at the Command of Allāh سبحانه وتعالى.

After him, will come before Allāh سبحانه وتعالى one who was blessed with much wealth, and Allāh سبحانه وتعالى will say, "Did I not give you plenty of wealth? What did you do with it?" He will say, "My Lord, I spent all my wealth in Your Way." "You are a liar" Allāh سبحانه وتعالى will remark. "You wished that men should say that such a one was very generous; and that has been already said." He will also be thrown into the Hell Fire.

So, from this, we learn that the only act that will be of any advantage to us with Allāh سبحانه وتعالى is the one which is performed with a pure intention. In the vocabulary of the Qur'ān and *Ḥadīth* this sincerity is known as *'Ikhlāṣ*.

The world in which we live and carry out our duties is a visible one, and our experience here is limited to that which we see and touch. In this world, we can form a good or bad opinion of someone just on the basis of their outward behavior. We are incapable of knowing the real intention behind a person's actions and the hidden secrets in people's hearts.

So it is said by `Umar ﷺ the Second *Khalīfah*, "Our job is to decide according to what is seen and the hidden secrets are left to Allāh ﷻ." In the Hereafter, Judgement will rest with the Lord, the Knower of the visible and invisible, Who will decide reward and punishment according to people's intentions.

This *Ḥadīth* has been transmitted by both 'Imām Bukhārī and 'Imām Muslim through their respective *'Isnād* (chain of transmitters) going back to Rasūlullāh ﷺ, in their two *Ṣaḥiḥain*, *Ṣaḥīḥ al-Bukhārī* and *Ṣaḥīḥ Muslim*, which are the most authentic collections on *Ḥadīth*.

* * * * * * * * * * * * * * * *

Exercise:

1. Write the *Ḥadīth* from page 38 in Arabic and give a brief explanation of its meaning.

2. "Allāh ﷻ sees intentions along with actions. He judges the worth and value of a deed by the motive with which it is performed." How can you support this view by the words of Rasūlullāh ﷺ?

3. Write a short paragraph on each of the following:

   a) *`Umar 'Ibn Al-Khaṭṭāb* رضي الله عنه
   b) *'Imām Bukhārī*

CHAPTER 8

PRINCIPAL TENETS OF ISLAM AND FAITH

Ḥadīth 1

عَنْ عَبْدِ ٱللَّهِ بْنِ عُمَرَ بْنِ ٱلخَطَّابِ رَضِيَ ٱللَّهُ عَنْهُمَا قَالَ: سَمِعْتُ رَسُولَ ٱللَّهِ صَلَّىٰ ٱللَّهُ عَلَيْهِ وَسَلَّمَ يَقُولُ: " بُنِيَ ٱلإِسْلاَمُ عَلَىٰ خَمْسٍ: شَهَادَةِ أَنْ لاَ إِلٰهَ إِلاَّ ٱللَّهُ وَأَنَّ مُحَمَّداً رَسُولُ ٱللَّهِ، وَإِقَامِ ٱلصَّلاَةِ، وَإِيْتَاءِ ٱلزَّكَاةِ، وَحَجِّ ٱلبَيْتِ، وَصَوْمِ رَمَضَانَ " .

(رَوَاهُ ٱلبُخَارِي وَمُسْلِمٌ)

Transliteration

`An `Abdillāhi 'Ibni `Umara 'Ibni-(a)l-Khaṭṭābi Raḍiya-(A)llāhu `an-humā qāla: Sami`tu Rasūu l(a)-Allāhi, Ṣalla-(A)llāhu `alai-hi wa-Sallama, yaqūlu: "Buniya-(a)l-Islāmu `alā Khamsin; Shahādati 'an lā 'ilāha 'ill(a)-Allāhu wa-'anna Muhammadan Rasūlu-(A)llāhi wa-'iqāmi (a)ṣ-Ṣalāti wa 'ītā'i-(a)z-Zakāti wa-Ḥajji-(a)l-baiti, wa-Ṣawmi Ramaḍāna."

(Rawāhu Al-Bukhārī wa-Muslim)

Translation

`Abdullāh 'Ibn `Umar 'Ibn Al-Khaṭṭāb (May Allāh be Pleased with both of them) said that he heard the Messenger of Allāh, *Ṣalla-(A)llāhu `alai-hi wa-Sallam*, saying, "Islam is built on five duties; testifying that there is no god but Allāh and that Muḥammad is the Messenger of Allāh; performing the prayers (*Ṣalāh*); paying the *Zakāh*; making the pilgrimage to the House *(Ḥajj);* and fasting (*Ṣawm)* in *Ramaḍān*."

(*Narrated by Al-Bukhārī and Muslim*)

A. About the Reporter

`Abdullāh b. `Umar رضي الله عنه is the son of `Umar 'Ibn Al-Khaṭṭāb رضي الله عنه, the second *Khalīfah* of Islam. During most of his early life, he accompanied Rasūlullāh ﷺ at home and abroad. He is one of those who transmitted a large number of Traditions. Next to 'Abū Hūrairah رضي الله عنه comes the name of 'Ibn `Umar رضي الله عنه, who transmitted 2,630 *'Aḥādīth*. We have authentic reports that he had a written collection of *'Aḥādīth*. At least eight of his students wrote *'Aḥādīth* from him.

B. Explanation of the Text

'Imān comprises the belief that Allāh سبحانه وتعالى alone is worthy of worship and that Muhammad ﷺ is the Messenger of Allāh سبحانه وتعالى. Bearing witness to the Prophethood of Rasūlullāh ﷺ means belief that:

His mission is the end of all Prophethood, and there will be no Messengers or prophets after him. All of the earlier messengers predicted his coming, and with him, the process of Revelation is complete. To believe in him is to also believe in all the Prophets of Allāh سبحانه وتعالى.

The Qur'ān as the Final Revelation; it contains and perfects all of the earlier Revelations sent to humankind through the earlier Prophets. These Revelations give guidance that we should worship Allāh سبحانه وتعالى. Prophet Muhammad ﷺ through his sayings and practice has actually explained to us the teachings of all the revelations.

Besides the *Shahādah,* which provides the central pillar that holds up the whole structure of Islam, the four other pillars are: Prayer (*Ṣalāh*), Fasting (*Ṣawm*); Charity (*Zakāh*); and Pilgrimage (*Ḥajj*).

A Muslim has to pray five times a day: (i). before sunrise, (ii). between mid-day and afternoon, (iii). in the late afternoon (iv). immediately after sunset and (v). between the time when twilight ends and just before dawn. This ensures that a Muslim is not forgetful of his or her dependence on Allāh سبحانه وتعالى. A Muslim obtains hope and strength through this periodic remembrance of Allāh سبحانه وتعالى.

A Muslim must fast for one lunar month each year, daily from dawn until sunset. This month is called *Ramaḍān*. Physically, Muslims do not eat, drink or smoke when fasting. Spiritually, Muslims must stay away from all evil thoughts, actions and speech. In other words, Muslims try to realize their true selves by striving to realize within themselves some aspects of *Sirah* of Rasūlullāh ﷺ.

Charity (*Zakāh*) means that everything that a Muslim possesses belongs to Allāh سبحانه وتعالى and, therefore, any needy person should have a share in it. Thus, the Muslim should willingly and gladly help individuals and society when there is a need. As humans have never been free from some kind of need, an annual amount is collected out of a Mulsim's income and savings and given to the poor and needy.

Pilgrimage (*Ḥajj*) to Makkah represents the Muslim's temporary ending of all worldly differences and activities in total submission to Allāh سبحانه وتعالى. It also symbolizes the unity of the Muslim *'Ummah*, and the oneness of all humanity.

These four pillars of Islam are mixed with all aspects of a Muslim's individual and social behavior. By following these Commands of Allāh سبحانه وتعالى, and living a life of complete submission and surrender to His Will, one becomes a true Muslim.

Ḥadīth 2

عَنْ أَبِي هُرَيْرَةَ رَضِيَ ٱللَّهُ عَنْهُ، قَالَ: قال رَسُولُ ٱللَّهِ صَلَّىٰ ٱللَّهُ عَلَيْهِ وَسَلَّمَ: " اَلإِيمَانُ بِضْعٌ وَسَبْعُونَ شُعْبَةً فَأَفْضَلُهَا قَوْلُ لاَ إِلٰهَ إِلاَّ ٱللَّهُ وَأَدْنَاهَا إِمَاطَةُ ٱلأَذَىٰ عَنِ ٱلطَّرِيقِ وَٱلحَيَاءُ شُعْبَةٌ مِنَ ٱلإِيمَانِ ".

(رَوَاهُ ٱلبُخَارِي وَمُسْلِمٌ)

Transliteration

`An 'Abī Hurairata Raḍiya-(A)llāhu `an-hu qāla, qāla: Rasūlu-(A)llāhi, Ṣalla-(A)llāhu `alai-hi wa-Sallama: "Al-Imānu biḍ`un wa-sab`ūna shu`batan, fa-'afḍalu-hā qawlu lā 'ilāha 'ill(a)-Allāhu wa-'adnā-hā 'imāṭatu-(a)l-'adhā `ani

(a)ṭ-ṭarīqi wa-(a)l-ḥayā'u shu`batun mina (a)l-'Īmāni"
(Rawāhu 'al-Bukhārī wa-Muslim)

Translation

It is narrated by 'Abū Hurairah ﷺ that the Messenger of Allāh ﷺ said, "Faith is composed of seventy and more branches, of which the highest is belief in *Lā 'ilāha 'illa Allāhu* (to deny all gods but Allāh) and the lowest is the removal of an obstacle from the road and *'Al-Ḥayā'* is an integral part of Faith."

(*It is reported by Bukhārī and Muslim*)

A. About the Reporter

'Abū Hurairah ﷺ was one of the *Ṣaḥābah* ﷺ. He was very close to Rasūlullāh ﷺ and served him for many years. Out of all the *Ṣaḥābah*, he transmitted the largest number of Traditions; as many as 5,374. This is not actually the number of Traditions but the number of channels through which they were transmitted. The most recent research proves that the number of *'Aḥādīth* transmitted by him is only 1,236. He is known to have had books of *Ḥadīth* in his possession. At least nine students of 'Abū Hurairah ﷺ recorded *'Aḥādīth* from him.

B. Explanation of the Text:

The word *Al-Ḥayā'* has no exact meaning in English. It stands for an attitude and behavior in which all indecency is avoided and in which faithfulness, modest piety, politeness and chastity are observed.

The phrase "branches of faith" refers to the deeds, virtues and all that follow as a natural outcome of faith. The testimony of *Tawḥīd*, the Oneness of Allāh ﷻ has been described as the highest, while removal of an obstacle from a path is the lowest of the branches of faith. Now, whatever good or virtuous acts can be imagined between the two grades constitute the branches of faith, whether they belong to the Rights of Allāh سبحانه وتعالى or to the Rights of Humans.

Al-Ḥayā is a moral characteristic which acts as a preventive measure to numerous sins and follies. As such, there exists a special affinity between *Al-Ḥayā* and faith.

* * * * * * * * * * * * * * * *

Exercise 1:

1. What are the five pillars of Islam? Define charity (*Zakāh*) in a short paragraph.

2. What does the *Shahādah* mean in the Traditions?

3. Write a short paragraph on `Abdullāh 'Ibn `Umar رضي الله عنه.

Exercise 2:

1. Explain the term '*Al-Ḥayā*'. What do you understand by it?

2. How would you explain the 'Branches of Faith' in the *Ḥadīth*?

3. What do you know about the reporter of *Ḥadīth* No. 2? How many Traditions did he report in his lifetime?

CHAPTER 9

THE IMPORTANCE OF FIVE DAILY PRAYERS

Ḥadī<u>th</u> 1

مَالِكٌ عَنْ يَحْيَىٰ بْن سَعِيدٍ بَلَغَنِي أَنَّ أَوَّلَ مَا
يُنْظَرُ فِيهِ مِنْ عَمَلِ ٱلْمَرْءِ: ٱلصَّلاَةُ، فَإِنْ قُبِلَتْ
مِنْهُ نُظِرَ فِيمَا بَقِيَ مِنْ عَمَلِهِ وَإِنْ لَمْ
تُقْبَلْ مِنْهُ لَمْ يُنْظَرْ فِي شَيْءٍ مِنْ عَمَلِهِ
(رَوَاهُ مَالِك)

Transliteration

Mālikun: `An Yaḥyā 'Ibn Sa`īdin "balag<u>h</u>a-nī 'anna 'awwala mā yunẓaru fī-hi min 'a`māli (a)l-mar'i (a)s-Ṣalātu fa-in qubilat min-hu nuẓira fīmā baqiya min 'amāli-hi, wa-'in lam tuqbal min-hu lam yunẓar fī <u>sh</u>ai'in min a' māli-hī."
(Rawāhu Mālik)

Translation

Mālik said on the authority of Yahyā b. Sa`īd: "I have come to know that the prayer is the first deed of a man to be checked (on the Day of Judgement). Once it is accepted, the rest of his deeds would be looked into as well. But if it is not accepted, none of his other deeds would be looked into." *(Narrated by Mālik)*

Ḥadī<u>th</u> 2

عَنْ بُرَيْدَةَ عَنْ رَسُول ٱللَّهِ صَلَّىٰ ٱللَّهُ عَلَيْهِ وَسَلَّمَ قَالَ:

" اَلعَهْدُ بَيْنَنَا وَبَيْنَهُمُ ٱلصَّلاَةُ فَمَنْ تَرَكَهَا فَقَدْ كَفَرَ"

(رَوَاهُ ٱلتِرْمِذِي وَٱلنِسَائِي)

Transliteration

`An Buraidata `an Rasūli-(A)llāhi, Ṣalla-(A)llāhu `alai-hi wa-Sallama, qāla: 'Al-`ahdu baina-nā wa-baina-humu-(a)ṣ-Ṣalātu, fa-man taraka-hā fa-qad kafara.

(Rawāhu Tirmi<u>dh</u>ī and Nasā'ī)

Translation

Buraidah reported that the Messenger of Allāh ﷺ has said, "The pledge (promise) between us and the people is prayer. One who abandons it, does an act of disbelief. (*Reported by Tirmi<u>dh</u>ī and Nasā'ī*)

Ḥadī<u>th</u> 3

أَبُو مَالِكٍ ٱلأَشْجَعِيّ عَنْ أَبِيهِ قَالَ: كَانَ ٱلنَّبِيُّ صَلَّىٰ ٱللَّهُ عَلَيْهِ وَسَلَّمَ إِذَا أَسْلَمَ ٱلرَّجُلُ أَوَّلَ مَا يُعَلِّمُهُ ٱلصَّلاَةَ أَوْ قَالَ: " عَلَّمْهُ ٱلصَّلاَةَ ".

(رَوَاهُ ٱلطَّبَرَانِي)

Transliteration

'AbūMālikin Al-'Ashja`ī `an 'abī-hi Qala: "Kāna (a)n-Nabiyyu, Ṣalla-(A)llāhu `alai-hi wa-Sallama, 'idhā 'aslama-(a)r-rajulu 'awwala mā yu`allimu-hu-(a)ṣ-Ṣalāta, 'aw qāla, `allim-hu (a)ṣ-Ṣalāta.

(Rawāhu Tabarānī)

Translation

'Abū Mālik 'Al-Ashja`ī reported his father as saying; "Whenever a man accepts Islam, the very first thing Rasūlullāh ﷺ used to teach him was the prayer." *(Narrated by Ṭabarānī)*

Ḥadīth 4

عَنْ أَبِى ذَرٍّ أَنَّ ٱلنَّبِيَّ صَلَّىٰ ٱللَّهُ عَلَيْهِ وَسَلَّمَ خَرَجَ

فِي ٱلشِّتَاءِ وَٱلوَرَقُ يَتَهَافَتُ فَأَخَذَ بِغُصْنِ شَجَرَةٍ

فَجَعَلَ ٱلوَرَقُ يَتَهَافَتُ ، فَقَالَ : " يَا أَبَا ذَرٍّ ! " ،

قُلْتُ لَبَّيْكَ يَا رَسُولَ ٱللَّهِ، قَالَ: " إِنَّ ٱلعَبْدَ

ٱلمُسْلِمَ لَيُصَلِّي ٱلصَّلَاةَ يُرِيدُ بِهَا وَجْهَ ٱللَّهِ فَتَهَافَتُ عَنْهُ

ذُنُوبُهُ كَمَا تَهَافَتَ هٰذَا ٱلوَرَقُ مِنَ ٱلشَّجَرَةِ " .

(مُسْنَدُ أَحْمَد)

Transliteration

`An 'Abī Dharrin 'anna-(a)n-Nabiyya, Ṣalla-(A)llāhu `alai-hi wa-Sallama, kharaja fi-(a)sh-shitā'i wa-(a)l-waraqu yatahāfatu fa-'akhadha bi-ghusni-shajaratin fa-ja`ala-(a)l-waraqu yatahāfatu fa-qāla: "Yā 'Abā Dharrin!" qultu labbai-ka yā Rasūla-(A)llāhi qāla: "Inna-(a)l-`abda-(a)l-Muslima la-yuṣalli-(a)ṣ-ṣalāta yurīdu bi-hā Wajha-(A)llāhi, fa-tahāfatu `an-hu dhunūbu-hu ka-mā tahāfata hādha-(a)l-waraqu mina-(a)sh-shajarati."

(Musnad 'Aḥmad)

Translation

'Abū Dharr reported that Rasūlullāh ﷺ came out once in winter while the leaves were falling. He caught hold of the branch of a tree, causing its leaves to fall. Then he said, "O 'Abū Dharr," I replied: "Yes, O Messenger of Allāh?" He said, "When a Muslim prays sincerely to Allāh ﷻ his sins drop as these leaves have dropped from the tree." (*Musnad 'Aḥmad*)

Ḥadīth 5

وَعَنْ عَبْدِ اللَّهِ بِن عَمْرِ وابْنِ العَاص رَضِيَ اللّٰهُ
عَنْهُمَا أنَّهُ سَمِعَ رَسُولَ اللّٰهِ صَلَّى اللّٰهُ عَلَيْهِ وَسَلَّمَ
يَقُولُ: اِذَا سَمِعْتُم النِّدَآءَ فَقُولُوا مِثْلَ مَا يَقُولُ ثُمَّ
صَلُّوا عَلَيَّ فَانَّهُ مَنْ صَلَّى عَلَيَّ صَلٰوةً صَلَّى
اللّٰهُ عَلَيْهِ بِهَا عَشْرًا، ثُمَّ سَلُوا اللّٰهَ لِيَ الوَسِيْلَةَ ...
فَمَنْ سَأَلَ لِيَ الوَسِيْلَةَ حَلَّتْ لَهُ الشَّفَاعَةُ

(مُسْلِم)

Transliteration

`An `Abdullah ibn `Amar ibn al-`Āṣ, raḍiya (A)llāhu `an-humā anna-hu sami`a Rasūlullāhi, Ṣalla-(A)llāhu `alai-hi wa-Sallama, yaqulu: Idha sami`tumu (a)n-nida'a fa-qulu mithla ma yaqulu thumma ṣallu `alayya fa-inna-hū man ṣalla `alayya, ṣalla (A)llahu` alaihi-hi bi-ha `ashran, thumm salu (A)llaha liya (a)l-Wasīlata ....fa-man sa'ala liya (a)l-Wasīlata hallat la-hu (a)l-Shafā`ata

(Muslim)

Translation

`Abdullah Ibn `Amr ibn al-`Ās, may Allāh be pleased with both of them, reported that he heard the Messenger of Allāh, *Ṣalla-(A)llāhu `alai-hi wa-Sallam* say: When you hear the call (*Adhān*), repeat whatever he (the caller) says. Then send salutations upon me. Indeed, whoever invokes Allāh's blessings upon me, receives in return ten blessings from Allāh. Then ask Allāh to give me the *Wasīlah*....For if anyone asks *Wasīlah* for me, my intercession , *Shafā`ah,* for him becomes obligatory upon me. (*Muslim*)

A. About the Reporters

`Abdullāh b. `Amr b. Al-`Ās transmitted 700 *'Aḥādīth*. We know that he used to record *'Aḥādīth* while Rasūlullāh ﷺ was alive and entitled his books *Aṣ-Ṣaḥīfah Aṣ-Ṣādiqah*. At least seven of his students possessed *'Aḥādīth* from him in written form.

B. Explanation of the Text

The Qur'ān and *Sunnah* have laid great emphasis on offering prayer (*Ṣalāh*). The moment a person embraces Islam, the very first act he is taught is how to perform the

Ṣalāh. Prayer makes a clear distinction between a believer and a non-believer. A Muslim is expected to offer prayer five times a day. It is compulsory. One who intentionally gives it up without any real excuse, is committing an act of disbelief. The prayer forms a direct link between a Muslim and the Creator.

The Qur'ānic verses which a Muslim recites in the prayer five times a day reminds him of the purpose for which he was created. He recites in his prayer that all Praise and Thankfulness is for Allāh ﷻ alone; He is the Creator, the Sustainer, and the Ruler of the Universe. Allāh ﷻ is Kind and Merciful to His creatures. He has sent His Prophets and Messengers from time to time to guide humanity. We bow to Him alone and seek His guidance and help. A Muslim repeats several times in his daily prayer that Allāh ﷻ is the Master of the Day of Reckoning.

This fact creates a sense of responsibility in humans. The knowledge of this accountability in the Hereafter creates an awareness of our duty to God and other human beings. It means that we cannot forget our dependence on Allāh ﷻ and our duty to Him.

The last *Ḥadīth* speaks about the importance of responding to the call of prayer, sending salutations upon Rasūlullāh ﷺ and asking Allāh ﷻ to grant him the *Wasīlah*. The *Wasīlah* is a station closest to Allāh ﷻ.Rasūlullāh ﷺ requested his *'Ummah* to ask Allāh ﷻ to give that highest station to him. The Prophet ﷺ promises his *Shafā'ah* for those who do so. In fact, who else than Rasūlullāh ﷺ, who was the best human being, can be more deserving to receive that special place? By asking us to remember him in special prayers, he wants to show Allāh ﷻ how much his *'Ummah* loves him. He will return the love of his *'Ummah* through his love and his *Shafā`ah.*

* * * * * * * * * * * * * * * *

Exercise:

1. Show the importance of prayer in the first three *'Aḥādīth*.

2. How does prayer help in wiping out our sins?

3. What is *Wasīlah* and why should we ask this for Rasūlullāh ﷺ?

CHAPTER 10

LOVE OF RASŪLULLĀH ﷺ AS PART OF FAITH

Ḥadīth 1

عَنْ أَنَس بْنِ مَالِكٍ قَالَ، قَالَ ٱلنَّبِيُّ صَلَّىٰ ٱللَّهُ
عَلَيْهِ وَسَلَّمَ: " لاَ يُؤْمِنُ أَحَدُكُمْ حَتَّىٰ أَكُونَ أَحَبَّ
إِلَيْهِ مِنْ وَالِدِهِ وَوَلَدِهِ وَٱلنَّاسِ أَجْمَعِينَ ".

(مُتَّفَقٌ عَلَيْهِ)

Transliteration

`An 'Anas 'ibni Mālikin qāla: Qāla (a)n-Nabiyyu, Ṣalla-(A)llāhu `alai-hi wa-Sallama, "Lā yu'minū 'ahadu-kum ḥattā 'akūna 'aḥabba-'ilai-hī min wālidi-hī wa-waladi-hī wa-(a)n-nāsi 'ajma`īn"
(Muttafaqun `alai-hi)

Translation

'Anas b. Mālik ﷺ reported that Rasūlullāh ﷺ said: "None of you will have faith until I become more beloved to him ﷺ than his father, his children and all humankind." (*Agreed upon*)

Notes:

A. About the Reporter

'Anas b. Mālik's mother brought him to Rasūlullāh ﷺ when he was ten years old and left him there in the service of Rasūlullāh ﷺ. He served Rasūlullāh ﷺ for the next ten years. Rasūlullāh ﷺ once prayed for him, saying: *"O Allāh, bless him in his wealth and children and let him enter Paradise."*

'Anas رضي الله عنه is reported to have said when he was an old man: "I have seen two of Rasūlullāh's prayers about me answered, and I hope to see the third one." Owing to this prayer, he used to reap the harvest of wheat on his land twice a year. He died at the age of one hundred and three, in 91 A.H., and was survived by more than one hundred of his descendants. 'Abū Bakr رضي الله عنه, the first *Khalīfah* after Rasūlullāh ﷺ, had appointed `Anas to collect *Zakāh* from the province of Bahrain. He is among the nine foremost reporters of the Sayings of Rasūlullāh ﷺ and third after 'Abū Hūrairah رضي الله عنه and `Ā'ishah رضي الله عنها, the wife of Rasūlullāh ﷺ. According to the *Ḥadīth* collection of 'Imām 'Aḥmad (known as *Musnad 'Aḥmad*), the number of *'Aḥādīth* reported by him totals 2,178.

B. Explanation of the Text

In this *Ḥadīth*, love for Rasūlullāh ﷺ is regarded as a sign of faith itself. This love should be stronger than love for one's father, children or mankind. The three relations mentioned here remind us of three aspects of human affection, and show that a man should have more love for Rasūlullāh ﷺ than all other relations existing in his life. But how do you judge that your love for Rasūlullāh ﷺ is stronger than all other bonds? It is quite easy. Whenever you want to do something, just think of whether it agrees with the *Sunnah* of Rasūlullāh ﷺ or not. For example, in order to please his family and provide them with comfortable life, a father tries to earn more and more money, even by *Ḥarām* or unlawful means (like gambling, stealing selling alcohol or behaving dishonestly). If he truly loves Rasūlullāh ﷺ, he must abandon all prohibited activities disliked by Allāh ﷻ and Rasūlullāh ﷺ. Instead, he should be content with a simple life and earn his livelihood through lawful ways, to show his true love for Rasūlullāh ﷺ. Another common criterion is that of the daily prayers (*Ṣalāh*). A Muslim who delays his prayer and does not perform it at the appointed hour, without having a proper excuse, cannot claim to truly love Rasūlullāh ﷺ, who has declared the *Ṣalāh* to be the "comfort of his eyes."

The phrase "*Muttafaqun `Alai-hi*" (agreed upon) appears at the end of this *Ḥadīth*. This term is used in the study of *Ḥadīth* for those *'Aḥādīth* which have been transmitted by both Imām Bukhārī and 'Imām Muslim through their respective *'Isnād* (chain of transmitters) going back to Rasūlullāh ﷺ. This *Ḥadīth*, in particular, is also transmitted by 'Imām Nasā'ī.

'Imām Bukhārī compiled his famous collection of *Ḥadīth* after sixteen years of hard work. His collection contains about four thousand *'Aḥādīth,* excluding such *'Aḥādīth* repeated in various chapters of his book. It is recognized as the most authentic book after the Book of Allāh ﷻ by the entire Muslim *'Ummah*.

* * * * * * * * * * * * * * * *

Exercise:

1. Write *Ḥadīth* No.1 in Arabic and give a short explanation of its meaning.

2. What is meant by "*Muttafaqun`Alai-hi*" in the science of *Ḥadīth*?

3. Write a short biographical paragraph on 'Anas 'Ibn Mālik رضي الله تعالى عنه.

CHAPTER 11

DEATH AS A REMINDER OF THE NATURE OF THIS WORLD

Ḥadī<u>th</u> 1

عَنِ ٱبْنِ مَسْعُودٍ قَالَ: قَالَ ٱلرَّسُولُ صَلَّىٰ
ٱللَّهُ عَلَيْهِ وَسَلَّمَ: " كُنْتُ نَهَيْتُكُمْ عَنْ زِيَارَةِ
ٱلْقُبُورِ فَزُورُوهَا فَإِنَّهَا تُذَكِّرُ ٱلآخِرَةَ " .
(رَوَاهُ ٱبْنُ مَاجَةَ)

Transliteration

`An 'Ibni Mas`ūdin qāla: Qāla-(a)r-Rasūlu, Ṣalla-(A)llāhu `alai-hi wa-Sallama: "Kuntu nahaitu-kum `an ziyārati (a)l-qubūri fa-zūrū-hā fa-'inna-hā tu<u>dh</u>akkiru (a)l-'Ā<u>kh</u>irah."
(Rawāhu 'Ibn Mājah)

Translation

'Ibn Mas`ūd reported that the Messenger of Allāh ﷺ said, "I used to prohibit you from visiting cemeteries but do visit them (now) for they remind you of the Hereafter."
(*Narrated by 'Ibn Mājah*)

A. About the Reporter

`Abdullāh b. Mas`ūd ؓ embraced Islam in its early days. It is said that he is one of the first six who entered Islam. He also migrated to Abyssinia and fought in the battle of *Badr*.

He was lean and short in stature. He was one of the greatest jurists of his time. He held the post of judge in the city of Kūfah in Iraq. 'Ibn Mas`ūd ﷺ transmitted 748 *'Aḥādīth*. We have no information about his students who wrote down *'Aḥādīth* from him, but his own book was in the possession of his son. He migrated to Madīnah and died there in 32 A.H.

B. Explanation of the Text

In the beginning, Rasūlullāh ﷺ did not allow his followers to visit graveyards. Earlier generations had turned their cemeteries into places of worship. But later he allowed, and even encouraged, Muslims to visit the cemeteries because they remind people of the Hereafter.

Visiting cemeteries reminds us of the *'Ākhirah* (Hereafter), which is one of the basic concepts and fundamentals of the Islamic faith. The term *Al-'Ākhirah* tells us:

(a). That humans are not free to do whatever they want, but are answerable to Allāh ﷻ for all their conduct.

(b). That the present world is not everlasting, but will come to an end at an appointed hour known only to Allāh ﷻ.

(c). That when this world comes to an end, Allāh ﷻ will bring into being another world in which He will resurrect, at one and the same moment, all human beings ever born on earth. He will gather them together, examine their conduct and grant each one a just reward for his or her actions.

(d) That those who are considered good in Allāh's Judgement will be sent to Heaven, and those judged by Him as evil-doers will be sent to Hell.

(e) And that the real measure of success and failure is not one's wealth in this life, but one's success or failure according to God's Judgment in the next life.

Fear of Allāh ﷻ and worry about the Hereafter should play the most important role in the improvement of our faith. Rasūlullāh ﷺ made an effort to develop these two qualities in his followers.

Ḥadīth 2

عَنِ ٱبْنِ عُمَرَ رَضِيَ ٱللَّهُ عَنْهُمَا قَالَ: قَالَ ٱلرَّسُولُ
صَلَّى ٱللَّهُ عَلَيْهِ وَسَلَّمَ: " كُنْ فِى ٱلدُّنْيا
كَأَنَّكَ غَرِيبٌ أَوْ عَابِرُ سَبِيلٍ ".

(رَوَاهُ ٱلبُخَارِي)

Transliteration

`An 'Ibni `Umara, raḍiya-(A)llāhu `an-humā, qāla: Qāla (a)r-Rasūlu, Ṣalla-(A)llāhu `alai-hi wa-Sallama: "Kun fī (a)d-Dunyā ka'anna-ka gharībun 'aw `ābiru sabīlin."
(Rawāhu Al-Bukhārī)

Translation

It is reported by 'Ibn `Umar (may Allāh be pleased with them both) that the Messenger of Allāh ﷺ said: "Be in the world as though you were a stranger or a traveler."
(*Narrated by Al-Bukhārī*)

Explanation of the Text

The concept given to us about this life is that it is short and transitory. Here on this earth, we are given a period of time to live. During this time, we are being judged and tested by Allāh ﷻ. What we plant here in this life, we will reap in the next life. If we have as our motto: "eat, drink, and be merry, for tomorrow we die," and make this world our goal and devote and direct all our efforts and energies towards achieving it, we will forget the Hereafter and will definitely lose on the Day of Judgement.

It is this concept of the *Ākhirah* that determines the direction of our efforts and actions. Allāh ﷻ has given us a short span of life on this planet. Therefore, we should take advantage of this opportunity and not waste our time. Just as a traveler who does not make a motel that he is visiting his home, a true believer should not imagine this world to be his real home and not act as if he will live here forever.

Ḥadīth 3

عَنْ عَبْدِ ٱللَّهِ بْنِ عُمَرَ، قَالَ رَجُلٌ: يَا نَبِيَّ ٱللَّهِ، مَنْ أَكْيَسُ

ٱلنَّاسِ وَأَحْزَمُ ٱلنَّاسِ؟ قَال: " أَكْثَرُهُمْ ذِكْراً لِلْمَوْتِ

وَأَكْثَرُهُمُ ٱسْتِعْدَاداً لِلْمَوْتِ وَأُولَٰئِكَ ٱلأَكْيَاسُ

ذَهَبُوا بِشَرَفِ ٱلدُّنْيَا وَكَرَامَةِ ٱلآخِرَةِ ".

(رَوَاهُ ٱلطَّبَرَانِي)

Transliteration

`An `Abdillah 'Ibni `Umara, qāla rajulun: "Yā Nabiyy(a)-Allāhi! Man 'akyasu-(a)n-nāsi wa-'aḥzamu-(a)n-nās: Qāla, "Ak<u>th</u>aru-hum <u>dh</u>ikran li (a)l-mawti wa-'ak<u>th</u>aru-hum 'isti'dādan li (a)l-mawti wa-'ulā'ika (a)l-'akyāsu <u>dh</u>ahabū bi-<u>sh</u>arafi (a)d-Dunyā wa-karāmati (a)l-'Ā<u>kh</u>irati."

(Rawāhu Aṭ-Ṭabarānī)

Translation

`Abdullah b. `Umar ﷺ narrated that once a person said to Rasūlullāh ﷺ: "Oh Prophet of God! Tell me who is the wisest and most far-sighted of humans." Rasūlullāh ﷺ replied, "He who remembers death most and makes the greatest preparation for it. These wise and cautious people have earned respect in this world as well as glory in the Hereafter." (*Narrated by Ṭabarānī*)

Explanation of the Text

In this world, our standard of success is wealth, position, power and fame. We are often so busy in achieving these objectives, we forget that this life and its achievements are temporary, and that our real home is the Hereafter.

When we realize that the real life is the life of the Hereafter, it is obvious that the wisest and most farsighted among us are those who always keep death in mind and prepare for it. Actually, those who know that death is coming and yet do not prepare for it and remain surrounded in worldly pursuits and pleasures are the real losers.

About the Transmitter of this Ḥadī<u>th</u>

At-Tabarānī's family belonged to the Yemeni tribe La<u>kh</u>m, which migrated to Jerusalem and settled there. He was born in 260 A.H. He began studying *Ḥadīth* at an early age. He made long journeys for this purpose and visited Syria, Egypt, Yemen, Arabia, present day Iran and Afghanistan. He spent about 30 years in the learning of *Ḥadīth*, and the number of people he studied under exceeded one thousand. He died in 360 A.H.

He is one of those scholars who wrote a large number of books, but his most famous work is *Al-Mu`jam Al-Kabīr* in 12 volumes. This is an encyclopedia of *Ḥadīth* which contains not only *'Aḥādīth* of Rasūlullāh ﷺ, but a great deal of historical information as well. This book has completely or partially absorbed hundreds of books already published. Someone once asked him how he was able to gain so much knowledge and he replied, "By sleeping on straw mats for thirty years." Such was the simple and humble life he led in the Path of Rasūlullāh ﷺ.

* * * * * * * * * * * * * * * *

Exercise 1:

1. Why did Rasūlullāh ﷺ forbid his followers to visit cemeteries in the beginning,?

2. What do you understand by the term *'Al-'Ākhirah* ?

3. Write a short paragraph on 'Ibn Mas`ūd ﷺ.

Exercise 2:

1. Write *Ḥadīth* No. 2 in Arabic and give a brief explanation of its meaning.

2. Our life in this world is a test for us. Why? How would you explain this view in light of *Ḥadīth* No. 2?

Exercise 3:

1. Who are the wisest and the most farsighted among the people in this world? Explain using *Ḥadīth* No. 3.

2. Do you think the person who always remembers death and makes preparation for it earns respect in this world too? Explain.

CHAPTER 12

ON THE MERITS OF KNOWLEDGE

Ḥadī<u>th</u> 1

عَنْ عُثْمَانَ بْنِ عَفَّانَ رَضِيَ ٱللَّهُ عَنْهُ قَالَ: قَالَ رَسُولُ ٱللَّهِ صَلَّىٰ ٱللَّهُ عَلَيْهِ وَسَلَّمَ : " خَيْرُكُمْ مَنْ تَعَلَّمَ ٱلْقُرْآنَ وَعَلَّمَهُ ".

(رَوَاهُ ٱلْبُخَارِي)

Transliteration

`An `U<u>th</u>māna 'Ibni `Affāna, raḍiya-(A)llāhu `an-hu, qāla: qāla Rasūlu-(A)llāhi, Ṣalla-(A)llāhu `alai-hi wa-Sallama: "<u>Kh</u>airu-kum man ta`allama-(a)l-Qur'āna wa-`allama-hū."
(Rawāhu Al-Bu<u>kh</u>ārī)

Translation

It is narrated by `U<u>th</u>mān b. `Affān (May Allāh ﷻ be pleased with him) that the Messenger of Allāh ﷺ said, "The best among you is the one who has learned the Qur'ān and taught it to others." (*Related by Al-Bu<u>kh</u>ārī*)

About the Reporter

`U<u>th</u>mān b. `Affān ؓ was the third of the four *<u>Kh</u>ulafā' ar-Rā<u>sh</u>idah*. He became a Muslim in the early days of Islam. He was a very wealthy man and was a great financial help to the Muslims. He was very shy and modest. He served as the *Khalīfah* for twelve years and was murdered at the age of 82. A large number of people reported *'Aḥādīth* from him.

Ḥadīth 2

عَنْ أَنَس بْنِ مَالِكٍ قَالَ: قَالَ رَسُولُ ٱللَّهِ صَلَّىٰ ٱللَّهُ عَلَيْهِ وَسَلَّمَ: " طَلَبُ ٱلعِلْمِ فَرِيضَةٌ عَلَىٰ كُلِّ مُسْلِمٍ وَمُسْلِمَةٍ ".

(رَوَاهُ ٱبْنُ مَاجَةَ)

Transliteration

`An 'Anas 'ibni Mālikin qāla: Qāla Rasūlu-(A)llāhi, Ṣalla-(A)llāhu `alai-hi wa-Sallama: "Ṭalabu (a)l-`ilmi farīḍatun `alā kulli Muslimin wa-Muslimatin."

(Rawāhu 'Ibn Mājah)

Translation

It is narrated by 'Anas 'Ibn Mālik that the Messenger of Allāh ﷺ said, "The acquisition of knowledge is compulsory for every Muslim man and woman."

(*It is related by 'Ibn Mājah*)

Ḥadīth 3

عَنْ أَنَس بْنِ مَالِكٍ قَالَ: قَالَ رَسُولُ ٱللَّهِ صَلَّىٰ ٱللَّهُ عَلَيْهِ وَسَلَّمَ: " مَنْ خَرَجَ فِي طَلَبِ ٱلعِلْمِ فَهُوَ فِي سَبِيلِ ٱللَّهِ حَتَّىٰ يَرْجِعَ ".

(رَوَاهُ ٱلبُخَارِي)

Transliteration

`An 'Anas 'ibni Mālikin qāla: qāla Rasūlu-(A)llāhi, Ṣalla-(A)llāhu `alai-hi wa-Sallam: "Man kharaja fī ṭalabi-(a)l-`ilmi fa-huwa fī sabīli-(A)llāhi ḥattā yarji`a."

(Rawāhu At-Tirmidhi)

Translation

It is transmitted by 'Anas b. Mālik that Rasūlullāh ﷺ said, "Whoever sets out to seek knowledge is in the way of Allāh until he returns (home)."

(Related by At-Tirmidhi)

Ḥadīth 4

عَنْ أَبِي هُرَيْرَةَ قَالَ: قَالَ رَسُولُ ٱللَّهِ صَلَّىٰ ٱللَّهُ
عَلَيْهِ وَسَلَّمَ: " إِذَا مَاتَ ٱبْنُ آدَمَ ٱنْقَطَعَ عَمَلُهُ إِلاَّ
مِنْ ثَلاَثٍ: صَدَقَةٍ جَارِيَةٍ وَعِلْمٍ
يُنْتَفَعُ بِهِ وَوَلَدٍ صَالِحٍ يَدْعُو لَهُ ".

(رَوَاهُ مُسْلِمٌ)

Transliteration

`An 'Abī Hurairata qāla: Qāla Rasūlu-(A)llāhi, Ṣalla-(A)llāhu `alai-hi wa-Sallama,"'Idhā māta 'Ibnu 'Ādama 'inqaṭa`a `amalu-hu 'illā min thalāthin: Ṣadaqatin jāriyatin wa-`ilmin yuntafa`u bi-hi wa-waladin ṣālihin yad`ū la-hu."

(Rawāhu Muslim)

Translation

It is narrated by 'Abū Hurairah that Rasūlullāh ﷺ said, "When a man dies, his actions come to an end, with three exceptions: *Ṣadaqah Jāriyah* (recurring charity) knowledge from which benefit continues to be reaped, and the prayers of his pious children for him." *(Muslim)*

Explanation of the Text

Working hard to gain knowledge is required of every Muslim. The first word revealed to Rasūlullāh ﷺ was 'IQRA' (Qur'ān, 96:1) which means 'Read'. Therefore, the first Qur'ānic verses recited to Rasūlullāh ﷺ by angel Jibrīl عليه السلام commanded him to 'Read'. In other words, the very first teaching of Allāh سبحانه وتعالى was to read and spread knowledge. The Qur'ān enjoins upon every believer to observe, study, and contemplate the wonders of creation, which the Qur'ān calls (*'Āyāt Allāh*, the Signs of Allāh). The Qur'ān asks the believers to think, to know, and to ponder by asking: "*Do you not observe?*" "*Do you not think*?" and "*Do you not contemplate*?"

Rasūlullāh ﷺ himself used to teach the Qur'ān and his *Sunnah*. He ordered the *Ṣaḥābah* رضي الله عنهم to teach the Qur'ān and his *Sunnah* to those who could not, for certain reasons, be in his presence. "Pass on knowledge from me, even if it is only one sentence," he used to say. The same emphasis is noticeable in his last Farewell sermon at his last *Ḥajj* when he said:

Those who are present (here) should convey the message to those who are absent.

In the first *Ḥadīth* of this chapter, Rasūlullāh ﷺ said, "*The best among you is one who has learned the Qur'ān and then taught it to others.*"

The Qur'ān is the last authentic Revealed Book, sent down to the last in the line of Prophets. It is the Word of Allāh ﷻ, the Creator and Sustainer of the Universe. Rasūlullāh ﷺ always encouraged his *'Ummah* to seek knowledge and education and stated that gaining knowledge is compulsory for every Muslim. And the highest of all knowledge is the knowledge of Islam.

Again, Rasūlullāh ﷺ says that he who goes out in search of knowledge is striving hard in the way of Allāh ﷻ until he returns. In order to encourage learning and the acquisition of knowledge among his community, he spoke of great rewards in the Hereafter for the teacher and the students. Rasūlullāh ﷺ said:

"*If anyone pursues a path in search of knowledge, Allāh will thereby make easy for him the path to Paradise and the angels will spread their wings in pleasure for one who seeks knowledge, and all the inhabitants of the Heavens and the Earth, even the fish in the depths of the waters, ask forgiveness for him.*"

In this regard, Rasūlullāh ﷺ said, "*When a man dies, his acts come to an end, with three exceptions: Ṣadaqah Jāriyah (recurring charity), knowledge from which benefit continues to be reaped and the prayers of a good child for his or her parents."*

Ṣadaqah Jāriyah can be the building of a mosque, soup kitchen, school, hospital, or a charitable institution by which the community continuously benefits, even after the death of the person who had built it. This term is equally applicable to the knowledge a Muslim has left behind in the form of books, lectures, and the knowledge instilled in students taught during his or her lifetime.

* * * * * * * * * * * * * * * *

Exercise:

1. Write a short paragraph on `Uthmān b. `Affān ﷺ.

2. What importance did Rasūlullāh ﷺ give to the learning and the acquisition of knowledge? Explain it in light of the Traditions that you have studied.

3. Write *Ḥadīth* No. 3 in Arabic and give a brief explanation of it.

4. How would you explain the term "*Ṣadaqah Jāriyah*" in *Ḥadīth* No. 4?

CHAPTER 13

THE RIGHTS OF NEIGHBORS

Ḥadīth 1

عَنْ جَابِرٍ قَالَ: قَالَ رَسُولُ ٱللَّهِ صَلَّى ٱللَّهُ عَلَيْهِ وَسَلَّمَ: " اَلجِيرانُ ثَلاَثَةٌ: جَارٌ لَهُ حَقٌّ واحِدٌ وَجَارٌ لَهُ حَقَّان وَجَارٌ لَهُ ثَلاَثَةُ حُقُوق". فَأَمَّا ٱلَّذِي لَهُ حَقٌّ واحِدٌ فَجَارٌ مُشْرِكٌ لَهُ حَقُّ ٱلجَوار، وأَمَّا ٱلَّذِي لَهُ حَقَّان فَجَارٌ مُسْلِمٌ لَهُ حَقُّ ٱلإِسْلاَمِ وَحَقُّ ٱلجوارِ وأَمَّا ٱلَّذِي لَهُ ثَلاثَةُ حُقُوقٍ فَجَارٌ مُسْلِمٌ ذُو رَحِمٍ لَهُ حَقُّ ٱلإِسْلاَمِ وَحَقُّ الجِوارِ وَحَقُّ الرَّحِمِ.

(الجامع الصغير)

Transliteration

`An Jābirin qāla: Qāla Rasūlu-(A)llāhi, Ṣalla-(A)llāhu `alai-hi wa-Sallama: "Al-Jīrānu thalāthatun:Jārun la-hū ḥaqqun waḥidun, wa jārun la-hū ḥaqqāni, wa jārun la-hū thalāthatu ḥuqūqin; fa amma (a)lladhī la-hū ḥaqqun waḥidun fa-jārun mushrikun la-hū ḥaqqu (a)l-jawāri wa amma (a)lladhī la-hu ḥaqqani fa jārun Muslimun la-hu ḥaqqu (a)l-Islāmi wa ḥaqqu (a)l-jawāri. Wa amma (a)lladhī la-hū thalāthatu ḥuqūqin fa-jārun Muslimun dhū raḥmin la-hū ḥaqqu (a)l-Islāmi wa ḥaqqu (a)l-jawāri wa ḥaqqu (a)r-raḥami."

(Al-Jami` as-Ṣaghīr)

Translation

It is reported by Jābir that Rasūlullāh ﷺ, said, "Neighbors are of three kinds: one who enjoys only one right, the other who enjoys two, and still another one who enjoys three rights. As for the neighbor who enjoys but one right, he is the non-Muslim neighbor, he has the right of neighborhood. And as for one who has two rights, he is the Muslim neighbor; he has the right of Islam and the right of neighborhood. And as for one who has three rights, he is the Muslim neighbor who is a relative; he has the right of Islam, right of neighborhood, and the right of kinship." (*Related by 'Aḥmad in his Musnad*)

Notes:

About the Reporter

Jābir b. `Abdullāh ﷺ was one of the closest *Sahābah* of Rasūlullāh ﷺ. He joined the battle of *Badr*, the first decisive battle fought between the *Kuffār* and the Muslims. He transmitted 1,640 *'Aḥādīth*. At least fourteen of his students had his *'Aḥādīth* in written form.

Ḥadīth 2

عَنْ أَنَس قَالَ: قَالَ رَسُولُ ٱللَّهِ صَلَّىٰ ٱللَّهُ عَلَيْهِ وَسَلَّمَ: " لَيْسَ مِنَّا مَنْ بَاتَ شَبْعَانَ وَجَارُهُ جَائِعٌ " .

(رَوَاهُ ٱلطَّبَرَانِي فِي مُعْجَمِهِ)

Transliteration

`An 'Anas qāla: Qāla Rasūlu-(A)llāhi, Ṣalla-(A)llāhu `alai-hi wa-Sallama: "Laisa min-nā man bāta shab`āna wa-jāru-hū jā'i`un."

(Rawāhu Aṭ-Ṭabarāni fī Mu`jami-hi)

Translation

It is reported by 'Anas that Rasūlullāh ﷺ said, "He is not one of us (Muslims) who eats to his fill and enjoys a sound sleep at night while his neighbor goes hungry (and he is aware of it)." (*Mu`jam Aṭ-Ṭabarāni*)

Ḥadīth 3

عَنْ أَبِي هُرَيْرَةَ قَالَ: قَالَ رَسُولُ ٱللَّهِ صَلَّىٰ ٱللَّهُ عَلَيْهِ وَسَلَّمَ: " وَٱللَّهِ لاَ يُؤْمِنُ وَٱللَّهِ لاَ يُؤْمِنُ وَٱللَّهِ لاَ يُؤْمِنُ ، قِيلَ : مَنْ يَا رَسُولَ ٱللَّهِ؟ قَالَ: " ٱلَّذِي لاَ يَأْمَنُ جَارُهُ بَوَائِقَهُ ".

(رَوَاهُ ٱلبُخَارِي وَمُسْلِمٌ)

Transliteration

`An 'Abī Hurairata qāla: qāla Rasūlu-(A)llāhi, Ṣalla-(A)llāhu `alai-hi wa-Sallama: "Wa-(A)llāhi lā yu'minu, wa-(A)llāhi lā yu'minu, wa-(A)llāhi lā yu'minu." Qīla: Man yā Rasūla-(A)llāhi? qāla: "'Alladhī lā ya'manu jāru-hu bawā'iqa-hū."

(Rawāhu Al-Bukhārī wa-Muslim)

Translation

It is reported by 'Abū Hurairah that the Messenger of Allāh ﷺ said: "By God, he is not a true believer. By God, he is not a true believer. By God, he is not a true believer." Then he was asked, "Who is that, Oh Rasūlullāh?" He replied, "The one from whose mischief his neighbors do not feel safe." *(Al- Bukhāri and Muslim)*

Explanation of the Text

Islam is a complete way of life for humankind. It is a guidance both for the individual and for the society. Islam creates a balance between the individual and the society. An individual alone is accountable to Allāh ﷻ for his conduct and behavior in this world. Islam guarantees the fundamental rights of the individual and does not subscribe to the view that one must lose his individuality in society. On the other hand, it also awakens in humans a sense of social responsibility, organizes human beings both in a society and a state, and enjoins the individual to contribute to the good of the community.

A neighborhood is one of the most important institutions in our society. Islam has stressed the importance of family (parenthood), kinship, and neighborhood. When the institutions which give rise to a system break down, the whole order collapses.

Rasūlullāh ﷺ has attached great importance to the neighborhood. He exhorted his followers to safeguard the rights of neighbors, to the extent that he has declared good neighborliness to be an article of faith and a prerequisite to salvation and a measure of one's love for Allāh ﷻ and His Messenger.

In *Ḥadīth* No.1, Rasūlullāh ﷺ has divided neighbors into three categories: the neighbor with only one right is a non-Muslim, and as such, he is entitled only to the right of a neighbor. The neighbor with two rights is the neighbor who is a Muslim and as such he has a claim as a neighbor and as a Muslim brother. The neighbor with three rights is the neighbor who, in addition to being a neighbor and a Muslim, is also a relative, and as such, he will have one right as a neighbor, another as a Muslim and still another as a relative. In light of this Tradition, even the non-Muslims who are our neighbors have a claim to be offered help and sympathy.

In *Ḥadīth* No. 2, no distinction is made between a Muslim and a non-Muslim neighbor. In this Tradition, Rasūlullāh ﷺ excluded the man from his community who eats his fill while his neighbor, regardless of religion, goes hungry.

* * * * * * * * * * * * * * *

Exercise:

1. What are the three categories of a neighbor? Explain in the light of *Ḥadīth* No. 1.
2. Write *Ḥadīth* No. 2 in Arabic and give a short explanation of it.
3. Explain in a brief paragraph the concept of neighborhoods in light of the Traditions you have studied.

CHAPTER 14

CONTROLLING ANGER: A VIRTUE

Ḥadīth 1

عَنْ أَبِي هُرَيْرَةَ أَنَّ رَجُلاً قَالَ لِلنَّبِيِّ صَلَّى ٱللَّهُ عَلَيْهِ وَسَلَّمَ: أَوْصِنِي، قَالَ: " لاَ تَغْضَبْ ". فَكَرَّرَ ٱلسُّؤَالَ ثَلاَثَ مَرَّاتٍ ، وَكَرَّرَ ٱلرَّسُولُ ٱلجَوَابَ نَفْسَهُ .

(رَوَاهُ ٱلبُخَارِي)

Transliteration

`An 'Abī Hurairata 'anna rajulan qāla li (a)n-Nabiyyi, Ṣalla-(A)llāhu `alai-hi wa-Sallama, "Awṣinī": Qāla: "Lā taghḍab" Fa-karrara (a)s-su'āla thalātha marrātin wa-karrara (a)r-Rasūlu (a)l-jawāba nafsa-hu.

(Rawāhu Al-Bukhārī)

Translation

It was reported by 'Abū Hurairah that once a person said to Rasūlullāh ﷺ: "Give me a piece of advice." Rasūlullāh ﷺ replied; "Do not become angry." The man asked repeatedly, and each time Rasūlullāh ﷺ gave the same reply: "Do not become angry." *(Narrated by Al-Bukhārī)*

Explanation of the Text

Most Traditions are in the form of Rasūlullāh's talks and lessons in the company of his friends and followers. Others are in the form of replies to questions asked of him or instructions and warnings given in a particular situation.

In *Ḥadīth* No. 1, a person came to Rasūlullāh ﷺ and asked him for a piece of advice. Rasūlullāh ﷺ advised him to exercise self-control. Even the most mild-mannered person can lose his or her temper in certain situations. Therefore, this is the best advice possible. When a person loses his temper, he may also lose his senses and reason, and be unable to distinguish right from wrong. Under the influence of anger, a person is likely to commit mistakes and sins for which he or she must repent after regaining control.

Ḥadīth 2

عَنْ أَبِي هُرَيْرَةَ قَالَ: قَالَ رَسُولُ ٱللَّهِ صَلَّىٰ ٱللَّهُ عَلَيْهِ وَسَلَّمَ: " لَيْسَ ٱلشَّدِيدُ بِٱلصُّرَعَةِ إِنَّمَا ٱلشَّدِيدُ مَنْ يَمْلِكُ نَفْسَهُ عِنْدَ ٱلْغَضَبِ".

(رَوَاهُ ٱلْبُخَارِي وَمُسْلِمٌ)

Transliteration

`An 'Abī Hurairata qāla, qāla Rasūlu-(A)llāhi, Ṣalla-(A)llāhu `alai-hi wa-Sallama: Laisa-sh-shadīdu bi-(a)ṣ-ṣura`ati 'innama-(a)sh-shadīdu man yamliku nafsa-hu `inda-(a)l-ghaḍabi."
(Rawāhu Al-Bukhārī wa-Muslim)

Translation

It is narrated by 'Abū Hurairah that the Messenger of

Allāh ﷺ said, "The strong one is not he who can over-power his rival in wrestling, but rather he who keeps himself under control when roused to anger."
(Narrated in *Ṣaḥīḥ Bukhārī* and *Muslim*)

Explanation

A wrestler who struggles with a person and throws him to the ground is indeed considered powerful. In this Tradition however, a strong person is considered one who exercises self-control and keeps his emotions under control when angry. When anger overpowers a man, he often loses his reason and may break social and moral rules. To become angry or to lose one's temper is a natural emotion, but one should not lose control. Thus, a real wrestler is he who restrains himself when roused to anger and does not do anything that may be wrong or undesirable.

Ḥadīth 3

عَنْ عَطِيَّةَ بْنِ عُرْوَةَ قَالَ: قَالَ رَسُولُ ٱللَّهِ صَلَّىٰ ٱللَّهُ عَلَيْهِ وَسَلَّمَ: " إِنَّ ٱلْغَضَبَ مِنَ ٱلشَّيْطَانِ وَإِنَّ ٱلشَّيْطَانَ خُلِقَ مِنَ ٱلنَّارِ وَيُطْفَأُ ٱلنَّارُ بِٱلْمَاءِ فَإِذَا غَضِبَ أَحَدُكُمْ فَلْيَتَوَضَّأْ ".

(رَوَاهُ أَبُو دَاوُد)

Transliteration

`An `Aṭiyyata 'ibni `Urwah qāla: Qāla Rasūlu-(A)llāhi, Ṣalla-(A)llāhu `alai-hi wa-Sallam: 'Inna-(a)l-ghaḍaba mina-(a)sh-

Shaiṭāni wa-'inna (a)sh-Shaiṭāna khuliqa mina-(a)n-nāri wa-yuṭfau' (a)n-nāru bi (a)l-mā'i fa-'idhā ghaḍiba 'aḥadu-kum fal yatawaḍḍa'.

(Rawāhu 'Abū Dāwūd)

Translation

It is related by `Atiyyah b. `Urwah ﷺ that the Messenger of Allāh ﷺ said: "Anger is roused from the influence of Satan, and Satan has been created from fire, and fire is put out with water. So, when any of you is seized with anger, let him perform *Wuḍū'* (ablution).

(Narrated by 'Abū Dāwūd)

Explanation of the Text

In this Tradition, we are told that anger is roused by the influence of Satan. When a person loses his temper, he goes beyond the limits laid down by Allāh ﷻ and is under the influence of the Satan. In another Tradition Rasūlullāh ﷺ says:

"*When any of you is roused to anger, he should sit down if he is standing. If the anger subsides (as a result of it), well and good, but if does not, he should lie down.*"

In both Traditions quoted above, Rasūlullāh ﷺ has suggested ways to control our emotions and keep control over our feelings when provoked. It is more effective than all other methods of controlling one's feelings of anger. If a person keeps this *Ḥadīth* in mind when he is angry, and gets up and performs *Wuḍū'* thoroughly, his anger will subside and he will cool down.

* * * * * * * * * * * * * * *

Exercise:

1. Why did Rasūlullāh ﷺ repeat the answer to the question put to him three times?

2. Did Rasūlullāh ﷺ keep in mind the level of understanding of his followers when answering their questions? Explain it in light of *Ḥadīth* No. 1

3. How do you explain the word "Wrestler" in light of *Ḥadīth* No. 2.

4. "Anger is made under the influence of Satan" Explain this statement with *Ḥadīth* No. 3.

CHAPTER 15

PROPHETIC ADVICE FOR DEALING WITH OTHERS

Ḥadīth 1

عَنْ أَنَسٍ عَنِ ٱلنَّبِيِّ صَلَّى ٱللَّهُ عَلَيْهِ
وَسَلَّمَ قَالَ: " لاَ يُؤْمِنُ أَحَدُكُمْ حَتَّى
يُحِبَّ لِأَخِيهِ مَا يُحِبُّ لِنَفْسِهِ ".

(رَوَاهُ ٱلْبُخَارِي وَمُسْلِمٌ)

Transliteration
*`An 'Anasin `ani-(a)n-Nabiyyi, Ṣalla-(A)llāhu `alai-hi wa-
Sallama: Qāla: "Lā yu'minu 'aḥadu-kum ḥattā yuḥibba li-
'akhī-hi mā yuḥibbu li-nafsi-hi."*
(Rawāhu Al-Bukhārī wa Muslim)

Translation
It is reported by 'Anas ☙ that Rasūlullāh ☙ said, "A person cannot be a true Muslim unless he wants the same for his brother as he wants for himself."

(Narrated by Al-Bukhārī and Muslim)

Ḥadīth 2

عَنْ عَبْدِ ٱللَّهِ بْنِ عَمْرٍ عَنِ ٱلنَّبِيِّ صَلَّىٰ ٱللَّهُ
عَلَيْهِ وَسَلَّمَ قَالَ: " اَلْمُسْلِمُ مَنْ سَلِمَ ٱلْمُسْلِمُونَ
مِنْ لِسَانِهِ وَيَدِهِ وَٱلْمُهَاجِرُ مَنْ
هَجَرَ مَا نَهَىٰ ٱللَّهُ عَنْهُ ".

(رَوَاهُ ٱلْبُخَارِي)

Transliteration

`An `Abdillāhi 'ibni `Amrin `ani-(a)n-Nabiyyi, Ṣalla-(A)llāhu `alai-hi wa-Sallama, qāla: "Al-Muslimu man salima-(a)l-Muslimūna min lisāni-hi wa-yadi-hī, wa-(a)l-muhājiru man hajara mā naha-(A)llāhu `an-hu."

(Rawāhu Al-Bukhārī)

Translation

`Abdullāh 'ibni `Amr reported that Prophet ﷺ said, "A Muslim is the one from whose tongue and hand other Muslims are secure, and an emigrant (*Muhājir*) is the one who gives up what Allāh ﷻ has forbidden."
(*Narrated by Al-Bukhārī*)

Ḥadīth 3

عَنِ ٱلنُّعْمَانِ بْنِ بَشِيرٍ قَالَ: قَالَ رَسُولُ ٱللَّهِ صَلَّىٰ ٱللَّهُ عَلَيْهِ وَسَلَّمَ: " مَثَلُ ٱلْمُؤْمِنِينَ فِي تَوَادِّهِمْ وَتَرَاحُمِهِمْ وَتَعَاطُفِهِمْ مَثَلُ ٱلجَسَدِ إِذَا ٱشْتَكَىٰ عُضْوٌ مِنْهُ تَدَاعَىٰ لَهُ سَائِرُ ٱلجَسَدِ بِٱلسَّهَرِ وَٱلحُمَّىٰ".

(مُتَّفَقٌ عَلَيْهِ)

Transliteration

`Ani (a)n-Nu`māni 'ibni Bashīrin qāla: Qāla Rasūlu-(A)llāhi Ṣalla-(A)llāhu `alai-hi wa-Sallama: "Mathalu (a)l-Mu'minīna fī tawāddi-him wa-tarāḥumi-him wa ta`āṭufi-him mathalu-(a)l-jasadi 'idhā ishtakā `uḍwun min-hu tadā`ā la-hu sā'iru (a)l-jasadi bi-(a)s-sahari wa-(a)l-ḥummā."

(Muttafaqun `Alai-hi)

Translation

`An-Nu`mān b. Bashīr reported that Rasūlullāh ﷺ said, "Muslims, in their mutual love, kindness and compassion, are like the human body; when one of its parts is in pain the entire body feels the pain in both sleeplessness and fever. (*Bukhārī and Muslim*)

About the Reporter

An-Nu`mān b. Bashīr was one of the younger *Ṣaḥābah*. He was eight years old when Rasūlullāh ﷺ died. Several people reported *'Aḥādīth* from him.

Ḥadī<u>th</u> 4

عَنْ عَبْدِ ٱللَّهِ بْنِ عَبَّاسٍ رَضِيَ ٱللَّهُ عَنْهُمَا قَالَ:
قَالَ رَسُولُ ٱللَّهِ صَلَّىٰ ٱللَّهُ عَلَيْهِ وَسَلَّمَ: " لَيْسَ
مِنَّا مَنْ لَمْ يَرْحَمْ صَغِيرَنَا وَلَمْ
يُوَقِّرْ كَبِيرَنَا".

(رَوَاهُ ٱلتِّرْمِذِي)

Transliteration

`An `Abdillāhi 'ibni `Abbāsin, raḍiya-(A)llāhu `an-humā, qāla: Qāla Rasūlu-(A)llāhi, Ṣalla-(A)llāhu `alai-hi wa-Sallama, "Laisa min-nā man lam yarḥam ṣa<u>gh</u>īra-nā wa-lam yuwaqqir kabīra-nā."

(Rawāhu At-Tirmi<u>dh</u>ī)

Translation

`Abdullāh 'ibni `Abbās رضي الله عنهما reported that Rasūlullāh ﷺ said, "He is not from us (i.e. he is not my follower) who has no mercy upon our younger ones and who does not respect our elders." (*Narrated by Tirmi<u>dh</u>ī*)

About the Reporter

\`Abdullāh b. \`Abbās رضي الله عنهما was one of Rasūlullāh's first cousins. He was three years old when Rasūlullāh ﷺ migrated to Madīnah, and at the time of the Prophet's death, he was about fifteen years old. He was a great scholar and Rasūlullāh ﷺ prayed , *"May Allāh endow him with wisdom and insight in Dīn (Religion)."* \`Umar رضي الله عنه, the Second *Khalīfah*, used to consult with him on important issues. \`Abdullāh b.\`Abbās رضي الله عنهما transmitted 1,660 *'Aḥādīth*. At least nine of his students had *'Aḥādīth* from him in written form.

Ḥadīth 5

عَنْ أَبِي هُرَيْرَةَ قَالَ: قَالَ رَسُولُ ٱللَّهِ صَلَّىٰ ٱللَّهُ
عَلَيْهِ وَسَلَّمَ: " إِيَّاكُمْ وَٱلْحَسَدَ فَإِنَّ ٱلْحَسَدَ يَأْكُلُ
ٱلْحَسَنَاتِ كَمَا تَأْكُلُ ٱلنَّارُ ٱلْحَطَبَ ".

(رَوَاهُ أَبُو دَاوُد)

Transliteration

\`An 'Abī Hurairata qāla: Qāla Rasūlu-(A)llāhi, Ṣalla-(A)llāhu \`alai-hi wa-Sallama: "'Iyyākum wa-(a)l-ḥasada fa-'inna-(a)l-ḥasada ya'kulu-(a)l-ḥasanāti kamā ta'kulu (a)n-nāru (a)l-ḥaṭaba."

(Rawāhu 'Abū Dāwūd)

Translation

'Abū Hurairah reported that Rasūlullāh ﷺ said, "Guard yourselves against envy for it eats up good deeds as fire eats up wood." (*Narrated by 'Abū Dāwūd*)

Ḥadīth 6

عَنْ وَاثِلَةَ بْنِ ٱلْأَسْقَعِ رَضِيَ ٱللَّهُ عَنْهُ قَالَ: قَالَ رَسُولُ ٱللَّهِ صَلَّى ٱللَّهُ عَلَيْهِ وَسَلَّمَ: " لَا تُظْهِرِ ٱلشَّمَاتَةَ لِأَخِيكَ فَيَرْحَمْهُ ٱللَّهُ وَيَبْتَلِيكَ ".

(رَوَاهُ ٱلتِّرْمِذِي)

Transliteration

`An Wāthilata 'ibni-(a)l'-Asqa`i raḍiya-(A)llāhu `an-hu qāla:
Qāla Rasūlu-(A)llāhi, Ṣalla-(A)llāhu `alai-hi wa-Sallama: "Lā tuẓhiri-(a)sh-shamātata li-'akhī-ka fa-yarḥam-hu-(A)llāhu wa-yabtalī-ka."
(Rawāhu At-Tirmidhī)

Translation

It is reported by Wāthilah b. Al-'Asqa` ﷺ that Rasūlullāh ﷺ said, "Do not be happy at the misfortune of your brother, for Allāh may save him from it and afflict you with it." (*Narrated by At-Tirmidhī*)

About the Reporter

Wāthilah b. Al-'Asqa` ﷺ was one of the *Ṣaḥābah* of Rasūlullāh ﷺ. He served Rasūlullāh ﷺ for three years.

Ḥadīth 7

عَنْ أَبِي هُرَيْرَةَ قَالَ: قَالَ رَسُولُ ٱللَّهِ صَلَّىٰ ٱللَّهُ عَلَيْهِ وَسَلَّمَ: " إِيَّاكُمْ وَٱلظَّنَّ فَإِنَّ ٱلظَّنَّ أَكْذَبُ ٱلْحَدِيثِ وَلاَ تَجَسَّسُوا وَلاَ تَحَسَّسُوا ".

(اَلْبُخَارِي وَمُسْلِمٌ)

Transliteration

`An 'AbīHurairata qāla: Qāla Rasūlu-(A)llāhi, Ṣalla-(A)llāhu `alai-hi wa-Sallama, "Iyyākum wa-(a)ẓ-ẓanna fa-'inna-(a)ẓ-ẓanna 'akdhabu-(a)l-ḥadīthi wa-lā tajassasū wa-lā taḥassasū."

(Al-Bukhārī wa-Muslim)

Translation

It is reported by 'Abū Hurairah that Rasūlullāh ﷺ said, "Beware of suspicion, for suspicion may be based on the most untrue information; do not spy upon one another, and do not try to find out each other's hidden faults." (*Al-Bukhārī and Muslim*)

Ḥadīth 8

عَنْ جَرِيرِ بْنِ عَبْدِ ٱللَّهِ قَالَ: قَالَ رَسُولُ ٱللَّهِ

صَلَّىٰ ٱللَّهُ عَلَيْهِ وَسَلَّمَ: " مَنْ يُحْرَمِ

ٱلرِّفْقَ يُحْرَمِ ٱلخَيْرُ كُلُّهُ ".

(أَبُو دَاوُد)

Transliteration

`An Jarīri 'ibni `Abdillāhi qāla: Qāla Rasūlu-(A)llāhi, Ṣalla-(A)llāhu `alai-hi wa-Sallama: "Man yuḥrami (a)r-rifqu yuḥrami (a)l-khairu kullu-hū."

('Abū Dāwūd)

Translation

Jarīr b. `Abdullāh ﷺ reported that Rasūlullāh ﷺ said, "Whoever is devoid of kindness and mercy is devoid of all goodness." (*'Abū Dāwūd*)

About the Reporter

Jarīr b. `Abdullāh ﷺ is one of the *Ṣaḥābah* of Rasūlullāh ﷺ. He entered the fold of Islam, forty days before the death of Rasūlullāh ﷺ. He settled down in the Iraqi city of Kūfah and remained there for many years. He died in 51 A.H. A large number of people reported *'Aḥādīth* from him.

Ḥadīth 9

عَنْ جَرِيرٍ قَالَ: قَالَ رَسُولُ ٱللَّهِ صَلَّىٰ ٱللَّهُ عَلَيْهِ وَسَلَّمَ: " لاَ يَرْحَمُ ٱللَّهُ مَنْ لاَ يَرْحَمُ ٱلنَّاسَ ".

(اَلْبُخَارِي وَمُسْلِمٌ)

Transliteration

`An Jarīrin qāla: Qāla Rasūlu-(A)llāhi, Ṣalla-(A)llāhu `alai-hi wa-Sallam(a), "Lā yarḥamu-(A)llāhu man lā yarḥamu (a)n-nās."
(Al-Bukhārī wa-Muslim)

Translation

It is reported by Jarīr that the Messenger of Allāh, *Ṣalla-(A)llāhu `alai-hi wa-Sallam(a)*, said, "Allāh will show no compassion to him who has no compassion towards human beings." (*Al-Bukhārī and Muslim*)

Explanation of the Text

Islam teaches the Unity of Allāh سبحانه وتعالى, the Unity of His creation and the Unity of revealed knowledge. Islam does not deny the Truth revealed in other religions but rather says that later followers changed some of that Truth with their own imaginations. Allāh سبحانه وتعالى sent our Prophet Muhammad ﷺ to purify His religion and bring it to final perfection. The message of Islam is for the entire human race and Allāh سبحانه وتعالى is the Lord of all the worlds. Rasūlullāh ﷺ is sent as a Mercy, not only for the Muslims but for the entire creation of Allāh سبحانه وتعالى.

In Islam, all humans are equal, whatever their color, language, race or nationality. It eliminates all the barriers of race, status and wealth. There can be no denying the fact that such barriers have always existed and do exist even today. Islam rejects all these distinctions and declares that the entire human race comes from a single pair of parents and forms one big family. Rasūlullāh ﷺ said:

"*All creatures of God form the family of God and he is the best loved by God who loves His creatures best.*"

All Muslims who submit and surrender to the Will of Allāh سبحانه وتعالى belong to one family. They are like real brothers and sisters to each other. The Believers should feel for each other so strongly that if anyone of them is afflicted with grief, they should considered it their own and be ready to help and share the distress and pain. People are to be respected not because of their race, status or wealth, but because they are good human beings.

Islam promotes love and respect. The younger and the junior should respect and obey the older, while the latter should be kind and compassionate towards the former. Lack of obedience and respect on the part of children and lack of mercy and kindness on the part of parents is one of the major causes of the breakdown of family life in the modern society of today. If mercy is removed from the human heart, one is deprived of all virtues and becomes a brute. Many good acts we perform have their roots, in fact, in kind-heartedness; a person who is not blessed with it has very little goodness in him. That is the reason why Rasūlullāh ﷺ has stressed the importance of showing kindness towards all human beings.

Rasūlullāh ﷺ laid great emphasis on mutual love and respect, and stressed the need for Mercy and Compassion towards all human beings. He forbade hatred, jealousy and fault finding. Rasūlullāh ﷺ condemned mutual suspicion, mistrust, scandal-mongering, back-biting and warned the *'Ummah* about their dire consequences. Such vices breed hatred and enmity and leave no room for good will and friendship.

* * * * * * * * * * * * * * *

Exercise:

1. Write short paragraphs on each of the following:

   i) `Abdullāh b. `Abbās ﷺ
   ii) Jarīr b. `Abdullāh ﷺ
   iii) Nu`mān b. Bashīr ﷺ

2. Write *Ḥadīth* No. 4 in Arabic and give a brief explanation of it.

3. "Whoever is devoid of mercy is deprived of all virtue." Explain this statement in light of *Ḥadīth* No. 8.

4. Explain the concept of Mercy in Islam from the Traditions you have studied.

5. What do you understand by the word *Muhājir*? Explain it using *Ḥadīth* No. 2

CHAPTER 16

ARROGANCE AND FALSE PRIDE CONDEMNED

Ḥadīth 1

عَنْ عَبْدِ ٱللَّهِ بْنِ مَسْعُودٍ قَالَ: قَالَ رَسُولُ ٱللَّهِ صَلَّىٰ ٱللَّهُ عَلَيْهِ وَسَلَّمَ: " لاَ يَدْخُلُ ٱلجَنَّةَ مَنْ كان فِي قَلْبِهِ مِثْقَالُ ذَرَّةٍ مِنْ كِبْرٍ"، فَقَالَ رَجُلٌ: " يَا رَسُولَ ٱللَّهِ، إِنِّي أُحِبُّ أَنْ يَكُونَ ثَوْبِي حَسَنًا، وَنَعْلِي حَسَنًا، أَفَمِنَ ٱلكِبْرِ ذَاكَ؟"، قَالَ: " لاَ، إِنَّ ٱللَّهَ جَمِيلٌ يُحِبُّ ٱلجَمَالَ . ٱلكِبْرُ بَطَرُ ٱلحَقِّ وَغَمْطُ ٱلنَّاسِ".

(رَوَاهُ مُسْلِمٌ وَٱلتِّرْمِذِي)

Transliteration

`An `Abdillāhi 'ibni Mas`ūdin qāla: Qāla Rasūlu-(A)llāhi, Ṣalla-(A)llāhu `alai-hi wa-Sallama: "Lā yadkhulu (a)l-Jannata man Kana fī qalbi-hi mithqālu dharratin min kibrin," " Fa-qāla rajulun: "Yā Rasūla-(A)llāhi, 'in-nī 'uḥibbu 'an yakūna thawbī ḥasanan wa-na`lī ḥasanan, 'afamina (a)l-kibri dhāka? Qāla "Lā 'inna-(A)llāha Jamīlun, yuḥibbu-(a)l-jamāla: Al-Kibru baṭaru-(a)l-Ḥaqqi wa ghamṭu (a)n-nāsi."

(Rawāhu Muslim wa At-Tirmidhī)

Translation

It is narrated by `Abdullah b. Mas`ūd that Rasūlullāh, *Ṣalla-(A)llāhu `alai-hi wa-Sallam(a)*, said: "He in whose heart is as much as a grain of false pride will not enter Paradise." A man remarked: "Oh Messenger of God! A man likes his garment to be beautiful and his sandals to be beautiful. Would it be considered as arrogance or haughtiness?" He replied: "No, not at all, indeed God is Beautiful and He loves beauty. Arrogance is to disregard what is right and true, and (secondly) to hold people in contempt."

(*Related by Muslim and At-Tirmidhī*)

Explanation of the Text

The theme of this Tradition is false pride and arrogance. The Qur'ān and the Traditions strongly condemn arrogance and pride. Instead, Islam teaches its followers humility and expects them to perform acts in a humble way. Pride is an exclusive attribute of Allāh سبحانه وتعالى which none can share with Him. In another *Qudsī* Tradition, Allāh سبحانه وتعالى informs us that, "*Pride is My cloak and Majesty is My lower garment, and I shall cause him who vies with Me regarding one of them to enter Hell.*" Islam does not believe in *hasab* (ancestral glory) or *nasab* (pedigree) and has wiped out these false concepts of honor and respect. The one who is most God-conscious is most honorable in the Sight of Allāh سبحانه وتعالى. All greatness is for Allāh سبحانه وتعالى Who is Eternal and Everlasting. Everything else is bound to perish sooner or later. In this Tradition, we are told that a vain and conceited person will not enter Paradise. Rasūlullāh ﷺ remarked that displaying beauty, however, should not be confused with arrogance and false pride. He further explains that Allāh ﷻ is Beautiful and loves beauty. The word 'Beauty' used in the Tradition covers all beautiful things of life.

In the end, Rasūlullāh ﷺ defined *'Al-Kibr'* or false pride, as disdaining or not submitting to what is true and right and despising people and thinking less of them.

* * * * * * * * * * * * * * *

Exercise:

1. Define and explain *'Al-Kibr'* (arrogance and false pride) in light of the Traditions you have studied.

2. How did Rasūlullāh ﷺ exactly define the word *'Kibr'*?

3. "Pride is an exclusive Attribute of Allāh ﷻ." Comment on this statement with special reference to the *Ḥadīth* mentioned above.

CHAPTER 17

EVERYONE HAS RESPONSIBILITIES

Ḥadīth 1

عَنْ عَبْدِ ٱللَّهِ بْنِ عُمَرَ قَالَ: قَالَ رَسُولُ ٱللَّهِ صَلَّىٰ ٱللَّهُ عَلَيْهِ وَسَلَّمَ: " كُلُّكُمْ رَاعٍ وَكُلُّكُمْ مَسْئُولٌ عَنْ رَعِيَّتِهِ، ٱلأِمَامُ رَاعٍ وَمَسْئُولٌ عَنْ رَعِيَّتِهِ، وَٱلرَّجُلُ رَاعٍ فِي أَهْلِهِ وَمَسْئُولٌ عَنْ رَعِيَّتِهِ، وَٱلْمَرْأَةُ رَاعِيَةٌ فِي بَيْتِ زَوْجِهَا وَمَسْئُولَةٌ عَنْ رَعِيَّتِهَا ، وَٱلخَادِمُ رَاعٍ فِي مَالِ سَيِّدِهِ وَمَسْئُولٌ عَنْ رَعِيَّتِهِ وَكُلُّكُمْ رَاعٍ وَمَسْئُولٌ عَنْ رَعِيَّتِهِ".

(مُتَّفَقٌ عَلَيْهِ)

Transliteration

`An `Abdillāhi 'ibni `Umara qāla: Qāla Rasūlu-(A)llāhi, Ṣalla-(A)llāhu `alai-hi wa-Sallama: "Kullu-kum rā`in wa-kullu-kum mas'ūlun `an ra`iyyati-hī, 'Al-'Imāmu rā`in wa-mas'ūlun `an ra`iyyati-hi, wa (a)r-rajulu rā`in fī 'ahli-hi wa mas'ūlun `an ra`iyyati-hi, wa (a)l-mar'atu rā`iyyatun fī baiti zawji-ha, wa mas`ūlatun `an ra`iyyati-ha wa (a)l-khādimu rā`in fī māli sayyidi-hi wa-mas`ūlun `an ra`iyyati-hi wa-kullu-kum rā`in wa-mas`ūlun `an ra`iyyati-hi."

(Muttafaqun `alai-hi)

Translation

`Abdullāh b. `Umar reported Rasūlullāh ﷺ saying, "Each of you is a shepherd and is responsible for his own flock. The *'Imām* or the leader who guides the people is a shepherd and is responsible for his flock; a man is a shepherd in charge of his family and he is responsible for his flock; a woman is a shepherdess in charge of her husband's house and children and she is responsible for them; and a servant is a shepherd in charge of his master's property and is responsible for it, so each of you is a shepherd and each of you is responsible for his flock." (*Bukhārī and Muslim*)

Explanation of the Text

This world is a place of test for us. Man is a viceregent or a representative of Allāh سبحانه وتعالى on this Earth. We have been given a fixed lifetime, during which we will be judged and tested. This world will come to an end and all of us will be resurrected on the Day of Judgement. All human beings will be accountable before Allāh سبحانه وتعالى and after being judged, we will be rewarded or punished for our good or bad deeds.

The Tradition explains the position and responsibilities of humans in this world. We live in a society and we have rights and obligations. We are responsible for the things that we are given charge of. If we do not carry out our duties according to the teachings of Rasūlullāh ﷺ and the Orders from Allāh سبحانه وتعالى, we will be sorry on the Day of Resurrection. Everybody, from the head of state to a servant, is responsible and answerable to Allāh سبحانه وتعالى for his or her actions.

* * * * * * * * * * * * * * * *

Exercise:

1. What concept of responsibility do you understand from this *Ḥadīth*?

2. *"Each of you is a shepherd and each of you is responsible for his flock."* Comment upon this statement in light of the *Ḥadīth*.

3. *"Man is a responsible being."* Explain it using this *Ḥadīth*.

CHAPTER 18

GOOD MANNERS REFLECT STRONG FAITH

Ḥadī<u>th</u> 1

عَنْ أَبِي هُرَيْرَةَ قَالَ: قَالَ رَسُولُ ٱللَّهِ صَلَّىٰ ٱللَّهُ

عَلَيْهِ وَسَلَّمَ: " أَكْمَلُ ٱلْمُؤْمِنِينَ

إِيمَانًا أَحْسَنُهُمْ خُلُقًا ".

(رَوَاهُ أَبُو دَاوُد)

Transliteration

`An 'Abī Hurairata qāla: Qala Rasūlu-(A)llāhi, Ṣalla-(A)llāhu `alai-hi wa-Sallama: "'Akmalu (a)l-Mu'minīna 'imānan 'aḥsanu-hum <u>kh</u>uluqan."

(Rawāhu 'Abū Dāwūd)

Translation

'Abū Hurairah related to us that the Rasūlullāh ﷺ said, "Muslims who show excellent behavior and manners are the most perfect in Faith." *(Narrated by 'Abū Dāwūd)*

Ḥadī<u>th</u> 2

عَنْ عَبْدِ ٱللَّهِ بْنِ عَمْرٍ قَالَ: قَالَ رَسُولُ ٱللَّهِ،

صَلَّىٰ ٱللَّهُ عَلَيْهِ وَسَلَّمَ: " إِنَّ خِيَارَكُمْ
أَحَاسِنُكُمْ أَخْلَاقاً ".
(رَوَاهُ ٱلْبُخَارِي وَمُسْلِمٌ)

Transliteration

`An `Abdillāhi ibni `Amrin qala: Qāla Rasūlu-(A)llāhi, Ṣalla-(A)llāhu `alai-hi wa-Sallama: "'Inna khiyāra-kum 'aḥāsinu-kum 'akhlāqan."

(Rawāhu Al-Bukhārī wa-Muslim)

Translation

It is related by `Abdullāh b. `Amr that the Messenger of God, *Ṣalla-(A)llāhu `alai-hi wa-Sallam(a)*, said, "The best among you are those who possess the best manners."

(*Narrated by Al-Bukhārī and Muslim*)

Ḥadīth 3

عَنْ أَبِي هُرَيْرَةَ، قَالَ: قَالَ
رَسُولُ ٱللَّهِ صَلَّىٰ ٱللَّهُ
عَلَيْهِ وَسَلَّمَ: " بُعِثْتُ لِأُتَمِّمَ
مَكَارِمَ ٱلْأَخْلَاقِ ".
(مُسْنَدُ أَحْمَد)

Transliteration

`An 'Abī Hurairata qāla: Qala Rasūlu-(A)llāhi, Ṣalla-(A)llāhu `alai-hi wa-Sallam(a), : "Bu`ithtu li-'utammima

makārima (a)l-'Akhlāqi."
(Musnad 'Aḥmad)

Translation

'Abū Hurairah reported that Rasūlullāh *Rasūlu-(A)llāhi, Ṣalla-(A)llāhu `alai-hi wa-Sallam(a),* said, "I have been sent to bring good behavior to the highest perfection." (*Musnad 'Aḥmad*)

Ḥadīth 4

عَنِ ٱبْنِ عُمَرَ قَالَ: قَالَ ٱلرَّسُولُ صَلَّىٰ ٱللَّهُ عَلَيْهِ وَسَلَّمَ:

" إِنَّ مِنْ أَحَبِّكُمْ إِلَيَّ أَحْسَنُكُمْ أَخْلَاقاً " .

(رَوَاهُ ٱلْبُخَارِي)

Transliteration

`Ani (i)bni `Umar, qāla: Qāla-(A)r-Rasūlu, Ṣalla-(A)llāhu alai-hi wa-Sallama, "Inna min 'aḥabbi-kum 'ilayya 'aḥsanu-kum 'akhlāqan."
(Rawāhu Al-Bukhārī)

Translation

It is reported by `Abdullah b. `Umar that Rasūlullāh ﷺ said, "The closest to me from among you are those who have the best manners." *(Narrated by Al-Bukhārī)*

Ḥadī<u>th</u> 5

عَنْ عَائِشَةَ قَالَتْ : قَالَ رَسُولُ ٱللَّهِ صَلَّىٰ ٱللَّهُ عَلَيْهِ وَسَلَّمَ: " اَللَّهُمَّ كَمَا حَسَّنْتَ خَلْقِي فَحَسِّنْ خُلُقِي".

(رَوَاهُ ٱلبُخَارِي)

Transliteration

\`An \`Ā'i<u>sh</u>ata qālat: Qāla Rasūlu-(A)llāhi, Ṣalla-(A)llāhu \`alai-hi wa-Sallama: "'Allāhumma kamā ḥassanta <u>kh</u>alqī fa-ḥassin <u>kh</u>uluqī."

(Rawāhu Al-Bu<u>kh</u>ārī)

Translation

\`Ā'i<u>sh</u>ah related that Rasūlullāh, *Ṣalla-(A)llāhu \`alai-hi wa-Sallam(a)*, used to pray, "Oh God! as You have made my body good, make my manners good as well." (*Narrated by Al-Bu<u>kh</u>ārī*)

Explanation of the Text

Islam places great emphasis on morals, manners, behavior, and conduct. Morality occupies a key position in the teachings of Rasūlullāh ﷺ. After faith and belief, great stress is laid upon manners and behavior. One of the main purposes of sending the Messenger of God ﷺ is to instill good manners and noble qualities in human beings.

Islam is not simply a religion, but it is a complete way of

life; and so it gives us a code of conduct and behavior as well as a set of rights and responsibilities for the individual and the society.

According to the Qur'ān and *Sunnah*, a Muslim should carry out his moral responsibility, not only to his parents, relatives and neighbors, but to all of humankind. Islam builds a higher system of morality so that humans can realize their greatest potential. It purifies the soul of all bad qualities. It encourages feelings of responsibility and fosters the capacity for self-control. It helps to develop kindness, generosity, mercy and sympathy towards all creatures.

The Traditions mentioned above shed light on the importance that Islam attaches to behavior and manners. As Rasūlullāh ﷺ himself has said, "*I have been sent by God to teach good manners.*" Moral values, in fact, play an important role in molding one's life. A person with good moral behavior will not only lead a happy contented life, but will also be a source of comfort to others. On the contrary, if a man's social conduct and manners are bad, his life will be devoid of real joy and peace and he will also make the lives of his relatives, friends and all others around him miserable. These are the immediate benefits he will receive in this world, while in the Hereafter, he is going to reap the richest harvest.

* * * * * * * * * * * * *_ * * *

Exercise:

1. How do you explain the importance Islam attaches to behavior in light of the Traditions you have studied in this chapter?

2. Write *Ḥadīth* No. 2 in Arabic and briefly explain its meaning.

3. "*Morality forms the basis of Islamic teachings.*" Comment on this statement in a short paragraph.

CHAPTER 19

ASPECTS OF ISLAMIC CHARITY
"*ṢADAQAH*"

Ḥadī<u>th</u> 1

عَنْ حُذَيْفَةَ، قَالَ: قَالَ رَسُولُ ٱللَّهِ صَلَّى ٱللَّهُ
عَلَيْهِ وَسَلَّمَ: " كُلُّ مَعْرُوفٍ صَدَقَةٌ ".

(رَوَاهُ أَبُو دَاوُدَ)

Transliteration

`An Ḥu<u>dh</u>aifata qala: Qāla Rasūlu-(A)llāhi, Ṣalla-(A)llāhu `alai-hi wa-Sallama: "Kullu Ma`rūfin Ṣadaqatun."
('Abū Dāwūd)

Translation

It is reported by Ḥu<u>dh</u>aifah that Rasūlullāh ﷺ said, "Every good (you do) is a Charity."

(*'Abū Dāwūd*)

About the Reporter

Hu<u>dh</u>aifah b. 'Al-Yamān ؓ was one of the *Ṣaḥābah* of Rasūlullāh ﷺ. `Umar b. Al-<u>Kh</u>aṭṭāb ؓ and `Alī b. 'Abi-Ṭālib ؓ reported *'Aḥādīth* from him. He died in 53 A.H. and was buried in Madīnah.

Ḥadī**th** 2

عَنْ أَبِي ذَرٍّ، قَالَ: قَالَ رَسُولُ ٱللَّهِ صَلَّىٰ ٱللَّهُ عَلَيْهِ وَسَلَّمَ: " لاَ تَحْقِرَنَّ مِنَ ٱلْمَعْرُوفِ شَيْئًا وَلَوْ تَلْقَىٰ أَخَاكَ بِوَجْهٍ طَلِيقٍ ".

(رَوَاهُ مُسْلِمٌ)

Transliteration

\`An 'Abī Dharrin qāla: Qala Rasūlu-(A)llāhi, Ṣalla-(A)llāhu \`alai-hi wa-Sallam: "Lā taḥqiranna mina-(a)l-ma\`rūfi shai'an wa-law talqā 'akhā-ka bi-wajhin ṭalīqin."

(Rawāhu Muslim)

Translation

'Abū Dharr reported that Rasūlullāh, *Ṣalla-(A)llāhu \`alai-hi wa-Sallam(a)*, said, "Do not consider even the smallest good deed as unimportant, even if its only meeting your brother with a cheerful face. (*Muslim*)

Ḥadī**th** 3

قَالَ أَبُو هُرَيْرَةَ عَنِ ٱلنَّبِيِّ صَلَّىٰ ٱللَّهُ عَلَيْهِ وَسَلَّمَ: "وَرَجُلٌ تَصَدَّقَ بِصَدَقَةٍ فَأَخْفَاهَا حَتَّىٰ لاَ تَعْلَمَ شِمَالُهُ مَا تُنْفِقُ يَمِينُهُ".

(رَوَاهُ اَلبَخُارِي)

Transliteration

Qāla 'Abū Hurairata `an-in-Nabiyyi, Ṣalla-(A)llāhu `alai-hi wa-Sallama:
"Wa-rajulun taṣaddaqa bi-ṣadaqatin fa-'akhfā-ha ḥattā la ta`lama
shimālu-hū mā tunfīqu yamīnu-hū."
(Al-Bukhārī)

Translation

'Abū Hurairah ﷺ said that Rasūlullāh, *Ṣalla-(A)llāhu `alai-hi wa-Sallam(a),* said, "There is a man who gives charity and he conceals it so much so that his left hand does not know what his right hand spends." (*Al-Bukhārī*)

Ḥadīth 4

عَنْ أَبِي هُرَيْرَةَ عَنِ ٱلنَّبِيِّ صَلَّىٰ ٱللَّهُ عَلَيْهِ وَسَلَّمَ:

" إِمَاطَةُ ٱلأَذَىٰ عَنِ ٱلطَّرِيقِ صَدَقَةٌ ".

(رَوَاهُ اَلبُخَارِي)

Transliteration

`An 'Abī Hurairata `an-in-Nabiyyi, Ṣalla-(A)llāhu `alai-hi wa-Sallama: "'Imāṭatu-(a)l-'adhā `ani-(a)ṭ-ṭarīqi sadaqatun."
(Al-Bukhārī)

Translation

'Abū Hurairah reported that Rasūlullāh, *Ṣalla-(A)llāhu `alai-hi wa-Sallam(a),* said, "Even removing from a path that which is harmful, is a charity." (*Al-Bukhārī*)

Ḥadīth 5

عَنْ أَبِي مُوسَىٰ ٱلأَشْعَرِيِّ قَالَ: قَالَ رَسُولُ ٱللَّهِ صَلَّىٰ ٱللَّهُ عَلَيْهِ وَسَلَّمَ: "عَلَىٰ كُلِّ مُسْلِمٍ صَدَقَةٌ". قَالُوا: فَإِنْ لَمْ يَجِدْ؟ قَالَ: "فَيَعْمَلُ بِيَدِهِ فَيَنْفَعُ نَفْسَهُ وَيَتَصَدَّقُ". قَالُوا: فَإِنْ لَمْ يَسْتَطِعْ أَوْ لَمْ يَفْعَلْ؟، قَالَ: "فَلْيَأْمُرْ بِٱلخَيْرِ". قَالُوا: فَإِنْ لَمْ يَفْعَلْ؟ قَالَ: "فَلْيُمْسِكْ عَنِ ٱلشَّرِّ، فَإِنَّهُ لَهُ صَدَقَةٌ".

(اَلبُخَارِي)

Transliteration

`An 'Abī Mūsa-(a)l-'Ash`arī qāla: Qala Rasūlu-(A)llāhi, Ṣalla-(A)llāhu `alai-hi wa-Sallama: "`Alā kulli Muslimin ṣadaqatun." Qālu: "fa-'in lam yajid?" Qāla: "Fa-ya`malu bi-yadi-hī fa-yanfa`u nafsa-hū wa-yataṣaddaqu." Qālū: "fa-'in lam yastaṭi` 'aw lam yaf``al." Qāla:"Fa-l ya'mur bi-(a)l-khairi." Qālu: "Fa-'in lam-yaf``al?" Qāla: "Fa-li-yumsik `ani-(a)sh-sharri, fa-'inna-hū la-hū ṣadaqatun."

(Al-Bukhārī)

Translation

'Abū Mūsā Al-'Ash`arī reported that the Messenger of Allāh, *Ṣalla-(A)llāhu `alai-hi wa-Sallam(a)*, said: "Every Muslim is obliged to give charity." They said: "But what if one does not have anything to give?" He said, "Then let him work with his own hands so he (first) benefits himself and then gives in charity." They said, "But if one is unable to do that?" He said: "So let him call (others) to do good." They said: "But if he is not able to do that?" He said, "So let him abstain from doing evil, for even that will be counted as his act of charity." *(Al-Bukhārī)*

Explanation of the Text

The word *`Ṣadaqah'* covers many things. It is not simply charity or alms-giving, but it has a wider meaning. *`Ṣadaqah'* in its literal sense refers to what you spend in the cause of Allāh ﷻ, or what a person sets aside from his wealth and gives voluntarily. But in light of the above Traditions, every good act you perform for the sake of Allāh ﷻ is *`Ṣadaqah'*. Even removing a harmful thing from the road is an act of charity. If a person cannot afford to spend on the poor and the needy, he should enjoin good and refrain from evil, for that would be *Ṣadaqah* for him. So much so that if he has nothing to give, he should at least meet his brother with a smile on his face.

* * * * * * * * * * * * * * * * *

Exercise:

1. Explain the concept of *Ṣadaqah.* Is it different from charity

2. How can a person, who does not have anything to give, participate in an act of charity?

CHAPTER 20

'AL-ḤAYĀ' (MODESTY): AN IMPORTANT ISLAMIC VIRTUE

Ḥadī<u>th</u> 1

عَنْ أَنَس بْن مَالِكٍ قَالَ : قَالَ رَسُولُ ٱللَّهِ صَلَّى ٱللَّهُ عَلَيْهِ وَسَلَّمَ: "إِنَّ لِكُلِّ دِينٍ خُلُقًا وَخُلُقُ ٱلاسْلاَمِ ٱلحَيَاءُ ".

(رَوَاهُ ٱبْنُ مَاجَة)

Transliteration

`An 'Anas ibni Mālikin qāla: Qāla Rasūlu-(A)llāhi, Ṣalla-(A)llāhu `alai-hi wa-Sallama: "'Inna li-kulli dīnin <u>kh</u>uluqan wa-<u>kh</u>uluqu (a)l-Islāmi-(a)l-Ḥayā'u."

(Rawāhu 'Ibn Mājah)

Translation

It is reported by 'Anas b. Mālik that the Messenger of Allāh, *Ṣalla-(A)llāhu `alai-hi wa-Sallam(a),* said, "Every religion has a distinctive quality, and the distinctive quality of Islam is modesty."
(*Narrated by 'Ibnu Mājah*)

Explanation

Al-Ḥayā' implies behavior in which all indecency is avoided and in which modest piety, purity, and chastity are observed.

This Tradition tells us that in every religion or faith, some particular aspect of moral behavior receives the highest attention and great emphasis is placed on it. Compassion and forbearance, for example, form the main point of the teachings of Prophet `Īsā (peace be upon him).

Ḥadīth 2

عَنْ عِمْرَانَ بْنِ حُصَيْنٍ قَالَ: قَالَ رَسُولُ ٱللَّهِ

صَلَّىٰ ٱللَّهُ عَلَيْهِ وَسَلَّمَ: " اَلحَيَاءُ لاَ يَأْتِي إِلاَّ

بِخَيْرٍ". وَفِي رِوَايَةٍ أُخْرَىٰ: " اَلحَيَاءُ خَيْرٌ كُلُّهُ ".

(مُتَّفَقٌ عَلَيْهِ)

Transliteration

`An `Imrāna ibni Ḥuṣainin qāla: Qāla Rasūlu-(A)llāhi, Ṣalla-(A)llāhu `alai-hi wa-Sallama: "'Al-Ḥayā'u lā ya'ti 'illa bikhairin" wa-fī riwāyatin 'ukhrā, "Al-Ḥayā'u khairun kullu-hū."

(Muttafaqun `Alai-hi)

Translation

It is reported by `Imrān b. Husain that the Messenger of Allāh, *Ṣalla-(A)llāhu `alai-hi wa-Sallam(a),* said that "Modesty brings nothing but good." In another version, "Modesty is everything good." (*Agreed Upon*)

Explanation

Generally, a person who does not respect his or her elders and behaves badly is considered arrogant. But even more disrespectful is the person who feels no shame before the Lord, and continues to say or do sinful and shameless acts, all the while knowing that Allāh سبحانه وتعالى sees and hears all that is said and done.

If a sense of modesty is alive and active in a person, his life will not only be pure in the sight of others, but he will not commit any act of disobedience with regard to the rules set by Allāh سبحانه وتعالى.

Ḥadī<u>th</u> 3

عَنِ ٱبْنِ عُمَرَ قَالَ: قَالَ رَسُولُ ٱللَّهِ صَلَّىٰ ٱللَّهُ
عَلَيْهِ وَسَلَّمَ :" إِنَّ ٱلحَيَاءَ وَٱلأِيمَانَ قُرِنَا جَمِيعًا
فَإِذَا رُفِعَ أَحَدُهُمَا رُفِعَ ٱلآخَرُ " .

(رَوَاهُ ٱلبَيْهَقِي)

Transliteration

`An 'Ibni `Umara qāla: Qāla Rasūlu-(A)llāhi, Ṣalla-(A)llāhu `alai-hi wa-Sallama! "'Inna-(a)l-Ḥayā'a wa (a)l-'Īmāna qurinā jamī`an fa-'i<u>dh</u>ā rufi`a 'aḥadu-humā rufi`a

(a)l-'ākharu."
(Al-Baihaqī)

Translation

It is related by `Abdullāh b. `Umar that the Messenger of Allāh, *Ṣalla-(A)llāhu `alai-hi wa-Sallam(a)* said, "Modesty and faith are companions; when one is taken away, the other goes too." (*Al-Baihaqī*)

Explanation of the Text

Faith and modesty are so deeply and closely linked that if one is present in an individual, so is the other. Modesty is a moral characteristic which acts to stop sins and misdeeds and as such, there exists a special bond between faith and modesty.

Ḥadīth 4

عَنِ ٱبْنِ مَسْعُودٍ قَالَ: قَالَ رَسُولُ ٱللَّهِ صَلَّىٰ ٱللَّهُ عَلَيْهِ وَسَلَّمَ: " إِنَّ مِمَّا أَدْرَكَ ٱلنَّاسَ مِنْ كَلَامِ ٱلنُّبُوَّةِ ٱلأُولَىٰ: " إِذَا لَمْ تَسْتَحِ فَٱصْنَعْ مَاشِئْتَ".

(رَوَاهُ ٱلبُخَارِي)

Transliteration

`An 'Ibni Mas`ūdin qāla, qāla Rasūlu-(A)llāhi, Ṣalla-(A)llāhu `alai-hi wa-Sallama: "'Inna mimmā 'adraka (a)n-nāsa min kalāmi(a)n-Nubuwwati-(a)l-'ūlā": "Idhā lam tastaḥi fa-(a)sna` mā shi'-ta."
(Rawāhu Al-Bukhārī)

Translation

'Ibn Mas`ūd said that the Messenger of Allāh, *Ṣalla-*

(A)llāhu `alai-hi wa-Sallam(a), has said: "Among the sayings of the previous prophets that came down to people is the saying, "if you do not feel shame, then do what you like." (*Narrated by Bukhārī*)

Explanation of the Text

This *Ḥadīth* is recognized as having two possible interpretations:

a). In matters where there is no guidance of the Revelation, a believer may act according to his conscience. A clear conscience of a believer tells him of what is right and what is wrong.

b). If one does not have a conscience and does not feel shame at wrongdoing, there is nothing to prevent him from misbehaving.

* * * * * * * * * * * * * * * *

Exercise:

1. List some acts of modesty you follow.
2. "*Modesty and faith exist together.*" Explain
3. Write *Ḥadīth* No. 4 in Arabic and explain it briefly.
4. What are the two possible interpretations of *Ḥadīth* No. 4? Explain in a brief essay.

CHAPTER 21

THE MERITS OF PATIENCE

Ḥadīth 1

عَنِ ٱبْنِ عُمَرَ قَالَ: قَالَ رَسُولُ ٱللَّهِ صَلَّىٰ ٱللَّهُ عَلَيْهِ وَسَلَّمَ:

" اَلـمُسْلِمُ ٱلَّذِي يُخَالِطُ ٱلنَّاسَ وَيَصْبِرُ عَلَىٰ أَذَاهُمْ أَفْضَلُ

مِنَ ٱلَّذِي لاَ يُخَالِطُهُمْ وَلاَ يَصْبِرُ عَلَىٰ أَذَاهُمْ " .

(رَوَاهُ ٱلتِّرْمِذِيُّ وَٱبْنُ مَاجَة)

Transliteration

`An 'Ibni `Umara qāla: Qāla Rasūlu-(A)llāhi, Ṣalla-(A)llāhu `alai-hi wa-Sallama: "'Al-Muslimu (a)lladhī yukhāliṭu (a)n-nāsa wa yaṣbiru `alā 'adhā-hum 'afḍalu mina-(a)lladhī lā yukhāliṭu-hum, wa-lā yaṣbiru `alā 'adhā-hum."

(Rawāhu At-Tirmidhī wa-'Ibn Mājah)

Translation

It is reported by 'Ibn `Umar that the Messenger of Allāh, *Ṣalla-(A)llāhu `alai-hi wa-Sallam(a),* said, "He who mixes with people and endures their harm, is better than he who does not mix with them and does not show patience, if he receives harm from them." (*At-Tirmidhī and 'Ibnu Mājah*)

Explanation of the Text

The literal meaning of *Ṣabr* is to exercise restraint (self-control), to keep oneself tied down. It also refers to will-power, firm resolve, and control over our desires. This enables us to advance along the path of Islam with total disregard for the temptations and obstacles. The Qur'ān says, "*seek help through ṣabr and prayer* (2:45)." The purpose of this order is to urge people to develop this quality.

This word has three meanings:

(a) patience and perseverance
(b) self-restraint
(c) constancy and steadfastness.

Ṣabr is our ability to accept Allāh's Will in sorrow, defeat or suffering, as opposed to complaining or rebelling.

Islam rejects withdrawl from the society. It urges Muslims to live in society and carry out our responsibilities towards our fellow beings. The practice of going into the wilderness and worshipping Allāh سبحانه وتعالى may have been found in earlier religions, but it is not (except in certain circumstances) a part of Islam. That is why, in this Tradition, we are told that a person who lives among the people and suffers but remains patient, is far better than a person who cuts himself off from the people and is at peace.

* * * * * * * * * * * *

Exercise:

1. What do you understand by *'Ṣabr'*? Relate an incident when you acted as a *Ṣābir*.

2. Write a brief explanation of the *Ḥadīth* about *Ṣabr* you have studied.

CHAPTER 22

HYPOCRISY CONDEMNED

Ḥadīth 1

عَنْ أَبِي هُرَيْرَةَ قَالَ: قَالَ ٱلرَّسُولُ صَلَّى ٱللَّهُ

عَلَيْهِ وَسَلَّمَ: " آيَةُ ٱلْمُنَافِقِ ثَلَاثٌ:

إِذَا حَدَّثَ كَذَبَ، وَإِذَا وَعَدَ

أَخْلَفَ، وَإِذَا ٱؤْتُمِنَ خَانَ " .

(مُتَّفَقٌ عَلَيْهِ)

Transliteration

`An 'Abī Hurairata qāla: Qāla-(a)r-Rasūlu, Ṣalla-(A)llāhu `alai-hi wa-Sallama: "'Āyatu (a)l-munāfiqi thalāthun: 'Idhā ḥaddatha kadhaba, wa-idhā wa`ada 'akhlafa wa-'idhā ' tumina khāna."

(Muttafaqun `alai-hi)

Translation

It is narrated by 'Abū Hurairah that the Messenger of Allah, *Ṣalla-(A)llāhu `alai-hi wa-Sallam(a)* said, "The signs of a hypocrite are three: whenever he speaks, he lies and whenever he makes a promise he breaks it and whenever he is trusted with something, he proves to be untrustworthy." (*Agreed upon: Al-Bukhārī and Muslim*)

Explanation of the Text

There emerged three classes of people when Rasūlullāh ﷺ started spreading Islam. There were the people who accepted Islam and believed in the Message with all of their heart. Then there were others who rejected the Message and another class of people called the hypocrites (*Munāfiqūn*). The hypocrites claimed to believe in Islam and pretended to be good and faithful Muslims. Yet in their hearts, they were not only unbelievers, but were bitter enemies of the Messenger of Allāh ﷺ and his Message. They used to tell lies and break promises. The *Ḥadīth* mentioned above tells us of the signs of a hypocrite.

* * * * * * * * * * * * * * *

Exercise:

1. What are the three signs of hypocrisy? Explain.

2. What were the three classes of people who emerged when Rasūlullāh ﷺ started inviting people to believe in Allāh سبحانه وتعالى?

3. Write the *Ḥadīth* in Arabic and explain it briefly.

CHAPTER 23

EXCHANGING GIFTS ENCOURAGED BY RASŪLULLĀH ﷺ

Ḥadīth 1

عَنْ عَائِشَةَ رَضِيَ ٱللَّهُ عَنْهَا عَنِ ٱلنَّبِيِّ صَلَّى ٱللَّهُ

عَلَيْهِ وَسَلَّمَ قَالَ: " تَهَادَوْا فَإِنَّ

ٱلْهَدِيَّةَ تُذْهِبُ ٱلضَّغَائِنَ " .

(رَوَاهُ ٱلتِّرْمِذِي)

Transliteration

`An `Ā'ishata, raḍiya-(A)llāhu `an-hā, `ani (a)n-Nabiyyi, Ṣalla-(A)llāhu `alai-hi wa-Sallama qāla: "Tahādaw fa-'inna (a)l-hadiyyata tudhhibu-(a)ḍ-ḍaghā'ina"

(Rawāhu At-Tirmidhī)

Translation

It is related by `Ā'ishah ؓ that Rasūlullāh, *Ṣalla-(A)llāhu `alai-hi wa-Sallam(a),* said, "Exchange presents with one another for it removes bad feelings from hearts." (*Narrated by At-Tirmidhī*)

Ḥadīth 2

عَنْ أَبِي هُرَيْرَةَ عَنِ ٱلنَّبِيِّ صَلَّىٰ ٱللَّهُ عَلَيْهِ وَسَلَّمَ قَالَ:

" تَهَادَوْا فَإِنَّ ٱلْهَدِيَّةَ تُذْهِبُ وَحَرَ ٱلصَّدْرِ وَلَا

تَحْقِرَنَّ جَارَةٌ جَارَتَهَا وَلَوْ شِقَّ فِرْسِنِ شَاةٍ ".

(رَوَاهُ ٱلتِّرْمِذِيُّ)

Transliteration

`An 'Abī Hurairata, `ani (a)n-Nabiyyi, Ṣalla-(A)llāhu `alai-hi wa-Sallama qāla: "Tahadaw fa-'inna-(a)l-hadiyyata tudhhibu waḥara (a)ṣ-ṣadri wa-lā tahqiranna jāratun jārata-hā wa-law shiqqa firsini shātin."

(Rawāhu At-Tirmidhī)

Translation

'Abū Hurairah related saying that the Messenger of Allāh, *Ṣalla-(A)llāhu `alai-hi wa-Sallam(a)* said, "Give presents to one another. Presents remove hatred from the hearts, and a lady neighbor should not even regard the gift of a part of a goat's hoof from her lady neighbor as one of no value. (*Reported by Tirmidhī*)

Explanation of the Text

In his Traditions, Rasūlullāh ﷺ has placed great emphasis on exchanging gifts with one another. Giving presents to each other promotes love and affection. It is also helpful towards the growth of friendly relations.

A gift is given as a token of goodwill and its purpose is to make the other happy and also to seek the pleasure of Allāh ﷻ. If a present is given to a person younger in age, it would be a gesture of affection; if to a friend, it would be a means to strengthening the bond of brotherhood; if to a needy person, it would be a source of comfort; and if to an elder, it would be a mark of regard and respect.

If something is given to a needy person for the sake of Allāh ﷻ with the intention of earning reward in the Hereafter, it would be charity (*Ṣadaqah*) not a gift (*Hadiyyah*). It is only when a gift is meant to be an expression of love, and through it the pleasure of Allāh ﷻ is to be sought, that it becomes a gift. If, however, a present is given with sincerity, the reward for it is no less than the reward for charity.

Rasūlullāh ﷺ accepted a *Hadiyyah* (gifts) with thankfulness and made use of it, while in case of a *Sadaqah* (charity) his practice was that he accepted it with gratitude and blessed the giver. However, he did not use for it himself but gave it to others.

* * * * * * * * * * * * * * * *

Exercise:

1. "*Giving presents to each other promotes mutual love and affection.*" Comment upon this statement of Rasūlullāh ﷺ.

2. What is the difference between a gift (*Hadiyyah*) and a charity (*Ṣadaqah*)?

3. Do you think that giving presents to one another in wipes out anger and bad feelings from our hearts? If so, give arguments to support your answer.

CHAPTER 24

PEOPLE WHO DESERVE SPECIAL CONSIDERATION

Ḥadī<u>th</u> 1

عَنْ أَبِي هُرَيْرَةَ قَالَ : قَالَ ٱلنَّبِيُّ صَلَّىٰ ٱللَّهُ عَلَيْهِ وَسَلَّمَ : " اَلسَّاعِي عَلَى ٱلأَرْمَلَةِ وَٱلمِسْكِينِ كَٱلمُجَاهِدِ فِي سَبِيلِ ٱللَّهِ أَوِ ٱلقَائِمِ ٱللَّيْلَ ٱلصَّائِمِ ٱلنَّهَارَ " .

(رَوَاهُ ٱلبُخَارِيُّ)

Transliteration

`An 'Abī-Hurairata qāla: Qāla (a)n-Nabiyyu, Ṣalla-(A)llāhu `alai-hi wa-Sallama: "As-sā`ī `ala-(a)l-'armalati wa (a)l-miskīni ka-(a)l-mujāhidi fī sabīli-(A)llāhi 'awi (a)l-qā'imi-(a)l-laila (a)ṣ-ṣā'ima (a)n-nahāra."

(Rawāhu al-Bu<u>kh</u>ārī)

Translation

'Abū Hurairah reported that Rasūlullāh, *Ṣalla-(A)llāhu `alai-hi wa-Sallam(a),* said, "One who makes efforts to help a widow or a poor person is like a warrior (*Mujāhid*) in the Path of Allāh, or like one who gets up for prayer in the middle of the night and fasts during the day."

(Reported by Al-Bu<u>kh</u>ārī)

Ḥadī<u>th</u> 2

عَنْ أَبِي هُرَيْرَةَ قَالَ: جَاءَ رَجُلٌ إِلَىٰ رَسُولِ ٱللَّهِ صَلَّىٰ ٱللَّهُ عَلَيْهِ وَسَلَّمَ فَقَالَ: " يَا رَسُولَ ٱللَّهِ، مَنْ أَحَقُّ بِحُسْنِ صَحَابَتِي؟ " قَالَ: " أُمُّكَ، قَالَ: " ثُمَّ مَنْ؟" قَالَ: " أُمُّكَ " ، قَالَ: " ثُمَّ مَنْ؟"، قَالَ: " أُمُّكَ " ، قَالَ: " ثُمَّ مَنْ؟" قَالَ: " أَبُوكَ " .

(رَوَاهُ ٱلْبُخَارِيُّ)

Transliteration

`An 'Abī Hurairata qāla: Jā'a rajulun ilā Rasūli-(A)llāhi, Ṣalla-(A)llāhu `alai-hi wa-Sallama, fa-qāla: "Yā Rasūla-(A)llāhi, man 'aḥaqqu bi-ḥusni ṣaḥābatī?" Qāla: "'Ummu-ka." Qāla: "Thumma man?" Qāla, "'Ummu-ka." Qāla "Thumma man?" Qāla: "'Umma-ka." Qāla: "Thumma man?" Qāla: "'Abū-ka."

(Rawāhu Al-Bukhārī)

Translation

'Abū Hurairah reported that once a person came to the Messenger of Allāh, *Ṣalla-(A)llāhu `alai-hi wa-Sallam(a),* and asked, "Messenger of God, who is the most deserving of friendly care from me?" He replied, "Your mother." He asked, "And then who?" and he replied, "Your mother." He asked, "And then who?" and he replied, "Your mother." He asked, "And then who?" He replied, "Your father."

(Narrated by Bukhārī)

Ḥadīth 3

عَنْ مُعَاوِيَةَ بْنِ جَاهِمَةَ أَنَّ جَاهِمَةَ جَاءَ إِلَى ٱلنَّبِيِّ صَلَّىٰ ٱللَّهُ عَلَيْهِ وَسَلَّمَ فَقَالَ: " يَا رَسُولَ ٱللَّهِ أَرَدْتُ أَنْ أَغْزُوَ وَقَدْ جِئْتُكَ أَسْتَشِيرُكَ" فَقَالَ: " هَلْ لَكَ مِنْ أُمٍّ؟"، قَالَ: " نَعَمْ "، قَالَ: " فَٱلْزَمْهَا، فَإِنَّ ٱلْجَنَّةَ تَحْتَ رِجْلَيْهَا " .

(رَوَاهُ ٱلنَّسَائِي)

Transliteration

`An Mu`āwiyata 'ibni Jāhimata, 'anna Jāhimata jā'a 'ila (a)n-Nabiyyi, Ṣalla-(A)llāhu `alai-hi wa-Sallama, fa-qāla: "Yā Rasūla-(A)llāhi: "'Aradtu 'an 'aghzuwa wa-qad ji'tu-ka 'astashīru-ka." Fa-qāla: "Hal la-ka min 'ummin?" Qāla: "na`am." Qāla: "Fa-(a)lzam-hā, fa-'inna (a)l-Jannata taḥta rijlai-hā."

(An-Nasā'ī)

Translation

Mu`awiyah, the son of Jāhīmah reported that Jāhīmah came to Rasūlullāh, *Ṣalla-(A)llāhu `alai-hi wa-Sallam(a),* and said, "I intend to join the fighting (in the Way of Allāh ﷻ) and I have come to seek your advice." Rasūlullāh ﷺ asked, "Do you have your mother?" He replied, "Yes." He said: "Stay with her and look after her for Paradise is at her feet." *(An-Nasā'ī)*

Ḥadī<u>th</u> 4

عَنْ أَبِي هُرَيْرَةَ قَالَ: قَالَ رَسُولُ ٱللَّهِ صَلَّىٰ ٱللَّهُ عَلَيْهِ وَسَلَّمَ: "

رَغِمَ أَنْفُ ثُمَّ رَغِمَ أَنْفُ ثُمَّ رَغِمَ أَنْفُ ". قِيلَ: مَنْ يَا

رَسُولَ ٱللَّهِ؟ قَالَ: " مَنْ أَدْرَكَ أَبَوَيْهِ عِنْدَ

ٱلكِبَرِ أَحَدَهُمَا أَوْ كِلَيْهِمَا فَلَمْ

يَدْخُلِ ٱلجَنَّةَ ".

(رَوَاهُ مُسْلِمٌ)

Transliteration

`An `Abī Hurairata qāla: Qāla Rasūlu-(A)llāhi, Ṣalla-(A)llāhu `alai-hi wa-Sallama: "Ra<u>gh</u>ima 'anfu, <u>th</u>umma ra<u>gh</u>ima 'anfu, <u>th</u>umma ra<u>gh</u>ima 'anfu," qīla: "Man yā Rasūla-(A)llāhi?" Qāla: "Man 'adraka abawai-hi `inda-(a)l-kibari, aḥada-humā, 'aw kilaihimā fa-lam yad<u>kh</u>uli (a)l-Jannata"

(Rawāhu Muslim)

Translation

It is related by 'Abū Hurairah that the Messenger of Allāh, *Ṣalla-(A)llāhu `alai-hi wa-Sallam(a),* said, "May he be humiliated; may he be disgraced; may he be brought low." "Who?" the *Ṣaḥābah* inquired. "The unfortunate person whose parents reached old age in his lifetime and he would not enter Paradise (by being kind and obedient to them)." (*Narrated by Muslim*)

Explanation of the Text

Before the advent of Islam, the Arabs used to bury their daughters alive. There was also no honor and respect in marriages. Sometimes, sons married their step-mothers after the death of their fathers. Most women lived miserable lives. They had no rights of inheritance. Islam raised the status of women in society and recognized their position as individuals who have different responsibilities but equal rights with men.

In *Ḥadīth* No. 1, we are told that a person who strives to help the widow and the poor is like a *Mujāhid* who fights in the Way of Allāh ﷻ. Often, when a woman's husband dies, the responsibility of earning for the children falls solely upon her shoulders. The problems of widows in many Eastern societies, where women do not typically go out to earn their livelihoods, are numerous. Widows in Hindu society have suffered tremendously. A widow is often made to burn herself alive on her dead husband's funeral pyre. Even today, in Hindu Society, a widow is not allowed to remarry. Rasūlullāh ﷺ upheld the cause of widows, by helping them encouraging their remarriage. In fact, he married a widow himself, thereby setting an example to be followed by all Muslims.

In Islam, a widow is encouraged to remarry, and one who helps the widow (by supporting her or marrying her) is like a *Mujāhid,* striving in the Path of Allāh ﷻ, or like one who stands up for prayer in the middle of the night (*at-tahajjud*) and fasts in the daytime.

In *Ḥadīth* No. 2, Rasūlullāh ﷺ has declared that the mother enjoys the greatest rights in human relationship and deserves the utmost care and attention. The claim of a mother is more than that of a father with respect to care and kind treatment. The Qur'ān also gives this right to mothers. In the Qur'an, the pain and suffering that the mother has to endure during pregnancy and childbirth and in bringing up the children has been mentioned, along with the command to show kindness to both parents.

In *Ḥadīth* No. 3, Rasūlullāh ﷺ told the *Ṣaḥābah* not to join the *Jihād* and advised him to look after his mother. He said that obedience to his mother would entitle him to Paradise.

It seems that Rasūlullāh ﷺ knew that the young man's parents needed the help of their son; that is why he asked him to go home and serve them, instead of going for *Jihād*.

This means that a son who does not take care of his parents in their old age and does not treat them with love and kindness will not enter *Jannah*.

* * * * * * * * * * * * * * *

Exercise:

1. How were women treated in the beginning of Rasūlullāh's mission?

2. How did Islam raise the status of woman in the society? Discuss in light of the Traditions you have studied on the subject.

3. Describe the rights and claims of a mother on her children. Explain these rights in light of *'Aḥādīth* No.2 and No.3.

CHAPTER 25

THE DUTY OF FIGHTING EVIL

Ḥadīth 1

عَنْ أَبِى سَعِيدٍ ٱلخُدْرِيِّ قَالَ: سَمِعْتُ رَسُولَ ٱللَّهِ صَلَّىٰ

ٱللَّهُ عَلَيْهِ وَسَلَّمَ يَقُولُ : " مَنْ رَأَىٰ مِنْكُمْ مُنْكَراً

فَلْيُغَيِّرْهُ بِيَدِهِ فَإِنْ لَمْ يَسْتَطِعْ فَبِلِسَانِهِ فَإِنْ

لَمْ يَسْتَطِعْ فَبِقَلْبِهِ

وَذٰلِكَ أَضْعَفُ ٱلأيمَانِ " .

(رَوَاهُ مُسْلِمٌ)

Transliteration

`An 'Abī Sa`īdin (a)l-Khudrīyyi qāla: sami`tu Rasūla-(A)llāhi, Ṣalla-(A)llāhu `alai-hi wa-Sallama yaqūlu: "Man ra'ā min-kum munkaran fal-yughayyir-hu bi-yadi-hi, fa-'in lam yastaṭi` fa-bi-lisāni-hi, fa-'in lam yastaṭi` fa-bi-qalbi-hi, wa-dhālika 'aḍ`afu (a)l-'Īmāni"

(Rawāhu Muslim)

Translation

It is reported by 'Abū Sa`īd Al-Khudri that he heard Rasūlullāh, *Ṣalla-(A)llāhu `alai-hi wa-Sallam(a)*, saying,

"Anyone among you who notices something evil should correct it with his own hand, and if he is not able to do so, then he should prohibit it with his tongue, and if he is not able to do so, he should at least consider it as bad in his heart, and that is the weakest of Faith, i.e the lowest degree of Faith."(*Narrated by Muslim*)

Explanation of the Text

It is an important duty of every Muslim to enjoin goodness and forbid evil. A Muslim should call people to the right path and accept the Supremacy of Allāh ﷻ and His Messenger ﷺ in all matters.

Individuals, the society, and the Islamic State, are all under obligation to put the Word of Allāh ﷻ into practice and to teach the Message of Islam to non-Muslims. In other words, an Islamic approach to life is a requirement of the Faith. Allah ﷻ says in the Qur'ān: "*Those whom, if We give them power in the land, establish the Ṣalāh and pay Zakāh and enjoin goodness and forbid evil* (*Al-Ḥajj* 22:41)."

In this Tradition, it is commanded that whenever anyone of us sees a wrong being committed, we should change it with our hand. This involves using whatever power we possess to change the situation. If we lack such authority, we can speak out and make a stand (even if it is only a symbolic one) against that wrong. If we cannot do that, then let us at least disapprove of it in our hearts, although that is the weakest degree of Faith.

* * * * * * * * * * * * * * * *

Exercise:

1. "*To enjoin goodness and forbid evil is one of the basic obligations for a Muslim.*" Write an essay explaining how we can fulfill this obligation.

2. Write the *Ḥadīth* in Arabic and explain it briefly.

CHAPTER 26

WHEN HOPE IS COMBINED WITH FEELING OF FEAR

Ḥadīth 1

عَنْ أَنَس بْنِ مَالِكٍ قَالَ: دَخَلَ رَسُولُ ٱللَّهِ صَلَّىٰ ٱللَّهُ عَلَيْهِ وَسَلَّمَ عَلَى رَجُلٍ مِنَ ٱلصَّحَابَةِ يَزُورُهُ فِي مَرَضِهِ فَقَالَ لَهُ: " كَيْفَ تَجِدُكَ يَا أَخِي"؟ ، قَالَ: " يَا رَسُولَ ٱللَّهِ، أَرْجُو ٱللَّهَ وَأَخَافُ مِنْ ذُنُوبِي". فَقَالَ رَسُولُ ٱللَّهِ: " مَا ٱجْتَمَعَ ٱلرَّجَاءُ وَٱلخَوْفُ فِي قَلْبِ مُسْلِمٍ إِلاَّ أَدْخَلَهُ ٱللَّهُ ٱلجَنَّةَ ".

(رَوَاهُ ٱلتِّرْمِذِيُّ)

Transliteration

`An 'Anas 'ibni Mālikin, qāla: dakhala Rasūlu-(A)llāhi, Ṣalla-(A)llāhu `alai-hi wa-Sallama, `alā rajulin mina (a)s-Ṣaḥābati yazūru-hu fī maraḍi-hi fa-qāla la-hu: "Kaifa tajidu-ka yā 'Akhī?" Qāla: "Yā Rasūla-(A)llāhi, 'arju-(A)llāha wa-'akhāfu min dhunūbī.
"Fa-qāla Rasūlu-(A)llāhi: "Ma (a)jtama`a-(a)r-rajā'u wa (a)l-khawfu fī qalbi Muslimin 'illā 'adkhala-hu (A)llāhu (a)l-Jannata."

(Jāmi` At-Tirmidhī)

Translation

"‘Anas b. Mālik reported that the Rasūlullāh, *Ṣalla-(A)llāhu `alai-hi wa-Sallam(a),* once visited a man who was sick. Rasūlullāh ﷺ said to him, "How do you feel, my brother? He replied, "O Messenger of God! My state is that I am hopeful of Divine Mercy, but, at the same time, there is fear of punishment for the sins I have committed." Rasūlullāh ﷺ remarked, "Be sure, in whose heart the feelings of hope and fear are present together, Allāh will surely bless him with Paradise."

(*Jāmi` At-Tirmidhī*)

Explanation of the Text

Rasūlullāh ﷺ visited one of his *Ṣaḥābah* during his illness. This Tradition tells us that one of the many rights and obligations a Muslim owes to his fellow Muslim is to visit him when he is ill and inquire after his health. In this Tradition, it is stated that the person might find himself in such a state of mind that, on the one hand, he is hopeful of Allāh's Mercy, and on the other he fears Allāh ﷾ for his sins. For these people Rasūlullāh ﷺ remarked that in whose hearts feelings of hope and fear are present at the time of illness and difficulties Allāh ﷾ will surely bless with Paradise.

A Muslim is asked to call upon Allāh ﷾ with fear and hope. This means that humans should fear Allāh ﷾ alone, and to Him alone should we look for the fulfillment of our wishes. While calling upon Allāh ﷾, we should realize that we are totally dependent on His favor and can attain success only if He helps and guides us to it. Similarly, we should also bear in mind that we can not succeed without Allāh’s support.

In *Sūrah Yūsuf*, Allāh ﷻ says, *"And never give up hope of Allāh's soothing Mercy: truly no one despairs of Allāh's soothing Mercy, except those who have no Faith (Yūsuf 12:87)."*

If a person is always hopeful of Divine Mercy, and has no fear of Allāh ﷻ, he is likely to slip and commit mistakes. He will be careless and negligent. On the other hand, if he is simply afraid of punishment for the sins he committed he will be disappointed of Allāh's Mercy. He will not perform any good or virtuous acts, thinking that he has already been doomed and cursed. Thus we see that the only proper combination in our hearts is the balance of fear and hope.

* * * * * * * * * * * * * * *

Exercise:

1. "*A Muslim is asked to call upon Allāh ﷻ with fear and hope.*" Comment upon this statement.

2. Write this Tradition in Arabic and explain it briefly.

CHAPTER 27

ASPECTS OF ISLAMIC MANNERS

Ḥadī<u>th</u> 1

عَنْ أَبِي هُرَيْرَةَ عَنِ ٱلنَّبِّي صَلَّىٰ ٱللَّهُ عَلَيْهِ وَسَلَّمَ

قَالَ : " يُسَلِّمُ ٱلرَّاكِبُ عَلَى ٱلمَاشِي

وَٱلمَاشِي عَلَى ٱلقَاعِدِ وَٱلقَلِيلُ

عَلَى ٱلكَثِيرِ وَٱلصَّغِيرُ عَلَى ٱلكَبِيرِ".

(مُتَّفَقٌ عَلَيْهِ)

Transliteration

`An 'Abī Hurairata `ani (a)n-Nabiyyi, Ṣalla-(A)llāhu `alai-hi wa-Sallama, qāla: "Yusallimu-(a)r-rākibu `ala (a)l-mā<u>sh</u>ī, wa (a)l-mā<u>sh</u>ī `ala (a)l-qā`idi wa (a)l-qalīlu `ala (a)l-ka<u>th</u>īri wa (a)ṣ-ṣa<u>gh</u>īru `ala (a)l-kabīri."

(Mutafaqun 'alai-hi)

Translation

'Abū Hurairah reported Rasūlullāh, *Ṣalla-(A)llāhu `alai-hi wa-Sallam(a)*, as saying: "One who is riding should greet the one who is walking, and the one who is walking should greet the one who is sitting, and a small company should greet a large one, and the younger should greet the older." (*Agreed upon*)

Ḥadīth 2

عَنْ عَبْدِ ٱللَّهِ بْنِ عَمْرٍ أَنَّ رَجُلاً سَأَلَ رَسُولَ ٱللَّهِ صَلَّىٰ ٱللَّهُ عَلَيْهِ وَسَلَّمَ: " أَيُّ ٱلاسْلاَمِ خَيْرٌ "؟ قَالَ: " تُطْعِمُ ٱلطَّعَامَ وَتَقْرأُ ٱلسَّلاَمَ عَلَىٰ مَنْ عَرَفْتَ وَمَنْ لَمْ تَعْرِفْ ".

(اَلبُخَارِي وَمُسلِمٌ وَأَبُو دَاوُد وَالنَّسَائِي وَأَبْنُ مَاجَة)

Transliteration

`An `Abdillāhi ibni `Amrin 'anna rajulan sa'ala Rasūla-(A)llāhi, Ṣalla-(A)llāhu `alai-hi wa-Sallama: "Ayyu (a)l-'Islāmi khairun?"

Qāla: "Tuṭ`imu (a)ṭ-ṭa`āma wa-taqra'u (a)s-salāma `alā man `arafta wa-man lam ta`rif."

(Al-Bukhārī, Muslim, 'Abu Dāwūd, (a)n-Nasā'ī wa 'Ibn Mājah)

Translation

`Abdullāh b. `Amr reported that when a man asked the Messenger of Allāh, *Ṣalla-(A)llāhu `alai-hi wa-Sallam(a),* which aspect of Islam was best, he replied: "That you should give food and greet with *Salām,* to those you know and to those you do not know."

(As-Sahihain, 'Abu Dā'ūd, Nasā'ī and 'Ibn Mājah)

Ḥadīth 3

عَنْ عَلِيٍّ قَالَ، قَالَ رَسُولُ ٱللَّهِ صَلَّىٰ ٱللَّهُ عَلَيْهِ وَسَلَّمَ:
" لِلْمُسْلِمِ عَلَى ٱلْمُسْلِمِ سِتٌّ بِٱلْمَعْرُوفِ : يُسَلِّمُ عَلَيْهِ إِذَا لَقِيَهُ،
وَيُجِيبُهُ إِذَا دَعَاهُ، وَيُشَمِّتُهُ إِذَا عَطَسَ، وَيَعُودُهُ إِذَا مَرِضَ،
وَيَتَّبِعُ جَنَازَتَهُ إِذَا مَاتَ، وَيُحِبُّ لَهُ مَا يُحِبُّ لِنَفْسِهِ ".

(رَوَاهُ ٱبْنُ مَاجَةَ وَٱلتِّرْمِذِي)

Transliteration

`An `Alīyyin qāla: Qāla Rasūlu-(A)llāhi, Ṣalla-(A)llāhu `alai-hi wa-Sallama: "Lil-Muslimi `ala-(a)l-Muslimi sittun bi (a)l-ma`rūfi: Yusallimu `alai-hi 'idhā laqiya-hu wa-yujību-hu 'idhā da`ā-hu wa-yushammitu-hu 'idhā `aṭasa wa-ya`ūdu-hu 'idhā mariḍa wa-yattabi`u janāzata-hu 'idhā māta wa-yuḥibbu la-hū mā yuḥibbu li-nafsi-hī.

(Rawāhu 'Ibn Mājah wa At-Tirmidhī)

Translation

`Alī reported Rasūlullāh, *Ṣalla-(A)llāhu `alai-hi wa-Sallam(a),* as saying, "A Muslim owes to a fellow Muslim six favors: he should salute him when he meets him; accept his invitation when he gives one; say "Allāh have mercy on you" when he sneezes; visit him when he is ill; follow his funeral procession when he dies and love for him what he loves for himself."

(Narrated by 'Ibnu Mājah wa At-Tirmidhī)

Ḥadīth 4

عَنْ قَتَادَةَ قَالَ: قُلْتُ لأَنَس: " أَكَانَتِ ٱلْمُصَافَحَةُ فِي أَصْحَابِ ٱلنَّبِيِّ صَلَّىٰ ٱللَّهُ عَلَيْهِ وَسَلَّمَ؟" قَالَ: " نَعَمْ " .

(رَوَاهُ ٱلبُخَارِي)

Transliteration

`An Qatādata, qāla, qultu li 'Anasin: "Akānati (a)l-muṣāfaḥatu fī Aṣḥābi-(a)n-Nabiyyī, Ṣalla-(A)llāhu `alai-hi wa-Sallama?" Qāla: "Na`am."

(Rawā-hu Al-Bukhārī)

Translation

Qatādah said, I asked 'Anas: "Did the *Ṣaḥābah* of Rasūlullāh ﷺ shake hands when they met? He replied: "Yes."

(*Narrated by Al-Bukhārī*)

Ḥadī<u>th</u> 5

عَنْ عُمَرَ بْنِ أَبِي سَلَمَةَ رَضِيَ ٱللَّهُ عَنْهُمَا قَالَ :

" كُنْتُ غُلاَماً فِي حَجْرِ رَسُولِ ٱللَّهِ صَلَّىٰ ٱللَّهُ عَلَيْهِ وَسَلَّمَ وَكَانَتْ يَدِي تَطِيشُ فِي ٱلصَّحْفَةِ، فَقَالَ لِي رَسُولُ ٱللَّهِ صَلَّىٰ ٱللَّهُ عَلَيْهِ وَسَلَّمَ:

" يَا غُلاَمُ، سَمِّ ٱللَّهَ وَكُلْ بِيَمِينِكَ وَكُلْ مِمَّا يَلِيكَ ".

فَمَا زَالَتْ تِلْكَ طِعْمَتِي بَعْدُ ".

(رَوَاهُ ٱلبُخَارِي)

Transliteration

`An `Umara 'ibni 'Abī Salamata raḍiyya-(A)llāhu `an-humā qāla: "Kuntu ghulāman fi ḥajri Rasūli-(A)llāhi, Ṣalla-(A)llāhu `alai-hi wa-Sallama, wa-kānat yadī taṭīshu fi (a)ṣ-ṣaḥfati fa-qāla lī Rasūlu-(A)llāhi, Ṣalla-(A)llāhu `alai-hi wa-Sallama: "Yā Ghulāmu, sammi-(A)llāha wa-kul bi-yamīni-ka wa-kul mimmā yalī-ka, "fa-mā zālat tilka ṭi`matī ba`du."

(Rawāhu Al-Bu<u>kh</u>ārī)

Translation

`Umar 'Ibn 'Abī Salmah ⬚ narrated: "I was a boy in the care of the Messenger of Allāh, Ṣalla-(A)llāhu `alai-hi wa-Sallam(a), and my hand was moving around in the bowl while eating. The Messenger of Allāh ⬚ said to me: "O boy, say Allāh's name (*Bismillāh*) and eat with your right hand and eat from the side nearest to you." This became my way of eating thereafter.

(Narrated by Al-Bukhārī)

Ḥadīth 6

عَنْ أَبِي سَعِيدٍ ٱلْخُدْرِيِّ قَالَ : كَانَ رَسُولُ ٱللَّهِ صَلَّىٰ

ٱللَّهُ عَلَيْهِ وَسَلَّمَ إِذَا فَرَغَ مِنْ طَعَامِهِ قَالَ:

" اَلْحَمْدُ لِلَّهِ ٱلَّذِي أَطْعَمَنَا

وَسَقَانَا وَجَعَلَنَا مُسْلِمِينَ ".

(رَوَاهُ مُسْلِمٌ)

Transliteration

`An 'Abī Sa`īdin-(a)l-Khudriyyi qāla, kāna Rasūlu-(A)llāhi, Ṣalla-(A)llāhu `alai-hi wa-Sallama, 'idhā faragha min ta`āmi-hi qāla: "Al-ḥamdu li-(A)llāhi-(a)lladhī 'aṭ`ama-nā wa-saqā-nā wa-ja`ala-nā muslimīna"

(Rawāhu Muslim)

Translation

'Abū Sai`īd Al-Khudrī ﷺ reported that the Messenger of Allāh, *Ṣalla-(A)llāhu `alai-hi wa-Sallam(a),* would say after finishing his meal, "*Al-ḥamdu li-(A)llāh* (All praise and thanks to Allāh ﷻ), Who fed us and provided us with drink and made us Muslims." *(Narrated by Muslim)*

Ḥadīth 7

عَنْ أَبِي قَتَادَةَ قَالَ: قَالَ رَسُولُ ٱللَّهِ صَلَّىٰ ٱللَّهُ عَلَيْهِ وَسَلَّمَ:

" إِذَا شَرِبَ أَحَدُكُمْ فَلاَ يَتَنَفَّسْ فِي ٱلإِنَاءِ".

(مُتَّفَقٌ عَلَيْهِ)

Transliteration

`An 'Abī-Qatādata qāla: Qāla Rasūlu-(A)llāhi, Ṣalla-(A)llāhu `alai-hi wa-Sallama: "Idhā shariba 'ahadu-kum fa-lā yatanaffas fi-(a)l'inā'i."

(Mutafaqun `alai-hi)

Translation

'Abū Qatādah said that Allāh's Messenger, *Ṣalla-(A)llāhu `alai-hi wa-Sallam(a),* said: "If any of you drinks water, let him not breath into the container." (*Agreed upon*)

Explanation of the Text

Islam is not merely a religion, based on codes and rituals. Rather, it is a complete way of life covering all the aspects of life. Islam provides guidance for all of life's issues. The Qur'ān tells people to enter into Islam and follow Allāh's Guidance in everything. Islam has provided a code of conduct for Muslims and Rasūlullāh ﷺ has taught true Islamic etiquette and manners through his own practice and sayings.

A Muslim should exchange greetings with other people, love those younger than him, and respect his elders. He has been taught by Allāh's Messenger ﷺ how to speak to others, how to eat, drink and sleep, etc.

A Muslim, when invited, should not refuse the invitation. He or she should pray for someone who is sneezing, visit friends who are ill and attend to their funerals when they die. Thus, Rasūlullāh ﷺ advised his followers of these things.

Apart from exchanging greetings with each other, Muslims are supposed to shake hands when they meet. This is an Islamic tradition which is practiced throughout most of the Muslim world. Shaking hands is symbolic gesture to show love and respect and to promote brotherhood.

* * * * * * * * * * * * * * *

Exercise:

1. "*Shaking hands and exchanging greetings with each other promotes love and respect.*" Comment upon the statement with reference to the Traditions you have studied.

2. Does Islam describe any code of conduct for Muslims? Explain in light of the *'Aḥādīth* mentioned above.

3. What does a Muslim owe to other Muslims? Explain it in light of *Ḥadīth* No. 3.

4. Write *Ḥadīth* No. 7 in Arabic and explain it briefly.

APPENDIX I

IQRA' TABLE OF TRANSLITERATION

q	ق	*	z	ز		'	أء	*
k	ك		s	س		b	ب	
l	ل		sh	ش		t	ت	
m	م		ṣ	ص	*	th	ث	*
n	ن		ḍ	ض	*	j	ج	
h	ه		ṭ	ط	*	ḥ	ح	*
w	و		ẓ	ظ	*	kh	خ	*
y	ي		'	ع	*	d	د	
			gh	غ	*	dh	ذ	*
			f	ف		r	ر	

SHORT VOWELS	LONG VOWELS	DIPHTHONGS
a \ ـَـ	a \ ـَا	aw \ ـَوْ
u \ ـُـ	u \ ـُو	ai \ ـَيْ
i \ ـِـ	i \ ـِي	
Such as: *kataba* كَتَبَ	Such as: *Kitab* كِتَاب	Such as: *Lawḥ* لَوْح
Such as: *Qul* قُلْ	Such as: *Mamnun* مَمْنُون	Such as: *'Ain* عَيْن
Such as: *Ni'mah* نِعْمَة	Such as: *Dīn* دِين	

* Special attention should be given to the symbols marked with stars for they have no equivalent in the English sounds .

ISLAMIC INVOCATIONS

Rasūlullāh, *Ṣalla Allahu 'alaihi wa Sallam* (صَلَّى ٱللَّهُ عَلَيْهِ وَسَلَّم), and the Qur'ān teach us to glorify Allāh when we mention His Name and to invoke His Blessings when we mention the names of His Angels, Messengers, the Ṣaḥābah and the Pious Ancestors.

When we mention the Name of Allāh we must say: *Subḥāna-hu Wa-Ta'ālā* (سُبْحَانَهُ وَتَعَالَى), Glorified is He and High.
In this book we write ﷻ to remind us to Glorify Allāh.

When we mention the name of Rasūlullāh ﷺ we must say: *Ṣalla Allāhu 'alai-hi wa-Sallam,* (صَلَّى ٱللَّهُ عَلَيْهِ وَسَلَّم), May Allāh's Blessings and Peace be upon him.
We write an ﷺ to remind us to invoke Allāh's Blessings on Rasūlullāh.

When we mention the name of an angel or a prophet we must say: *Alai-hi-s-Salām* (عَلَيْهِ ٱلسَّلَام), Upon him be peace.
We write an عليه السلام to remind us to involе Allāh's Peace upon him.

When we hear the name of the Ṣaḥābah we must say:
For more than two, *Radiy-Allahu Ta'ālā 'anhum,* (رَضِيَ ٱللَّهُ تَعَالَىٰ عَنْهُم), May Allāh be pleased with them.
For two of them, *Radiy-Allahu Ta'ālā 'an-humā* (رَضِيَ ٱللَّهُ تَعَالَىٰ عَنْهُمَا), May Allāh be pleased with both of them.
For a Ṣaḥābī, *Radiy-Allahu Ta'ālā 'an-hu* (رَضِيَ ٱللَّهُ تَعَالَىٰ عَنْهُ),For a Ṣaḥābiyyah, *Radiy-Allahu Ta'ālā 'an-hā* (رَضِيَ ٱللَّهُ تَعَالَىٰ عَنْهَا), May Allāh be pleased with her.
We write رضي الله عنه to remind us to invoke Allāh's Pleasure with a Ṣaḥābī or with Ṣaḥābah.

When we hear the name of the Pious Ancestor (*As-Salaf as-Ṣāliḥ*) we must say:
For a man, *Rahmatullāh 'alaihi* (رَحْمَةُ ٱللَّهِ عَلَيْه), May Allāh's Mercy be upon him.
For a woman, *Rahmatullāh 'alai-hā* (رَحْمَةُ ٱللَّهِ عَلَيْهَا), May Allāh's Mercy be with her.

APPENDIX III

GLOSSARY

A

***'adāb*:** (n) Islamic manners and behavior
***'aqīdah*:** (n) belief or creed
***'adl*:** (n) 1). justice; 2). righteous conduct
***aḥad*:** (a) singular; a *ḥadīth* whose narrators do not reach anywhere near the number for the *mutawatir* (continuous) *ḥadīth*.
***ākhirah*:** the Hereafter; the life beyond this transitory one

D

***ḍabt*:** (n) strong retentive memory; a necessary characteristic of the of the transmitters of Traditions
***ḍa'īf*:** (a) weak; a characterization of *ḥadīth* in which there is some defect either in the chain of trans mission or in perfect agreement with beliefs and practices

F

***fitnah*:** (n) temptation, discord, civil war, trial

H

***ḥadīth*:** (pl: *aḥādīth*): the recorded teachings, sayings and actions of Prophet Muhammad ﷺ which explain and interpret the Qur'ānic verses and Message of Islam
***hadiyyah*:** (n) gift
***ḥaj*:** (n) the pilgrimage to Makkah; one of the Five Pillars of Islam
***ḥasan*:** (a) the Good; a categorization of *ḥadīth* similar to *ṣaḥīḥ* except that some of its narrators are found to have defective memories in comparison to *ṣaḥīḥ*

narrators

ḥayā': an attitude and behavior in which all indecency is avoided, therefore acting as a preventive measure against numerous sins; as such, it serves to strengthen faith

ḥikmah: (n) 1). wisdom; 2). The Wisdom, the Qur'ānic term for the *Sunnah* of Rasūlallāh ﷺ

hijrah: (n) emigration; the *hijrah* to Madīnah from Makkah took place in 622 a.d.

ḥukm/ aḥkām: (n) a legal judgement, an ordinance, a decree; a verdict

I

'ibādat: (n) acts of worship

ikhlāṣ: extreme sincerity

isnād: (n) the chain of transmitters through whom the *ḥadīth* was transmitted

'ishārāt: signs of the Last Day

J

jāmī': (n) a comprehensive and inclusive reference book of *ḥadīth*

jihād: (n) striving in the way of Allāh سبحانه وتعالى

K

kibār: (n) false pride

kitāb: (n) 1). book; 2). The Book of Allāh سبحانه وتعالى (Al-Qur'ān)

khutbah: (n) sermon

khalīfah: (n) caliph

kufr: (n) denial of the Truth of Allāh سبحانه وتعالى; disbelief

M

manāqib: (n) virtues, outstanding traits; feats, exploits

mujāhid: (n) warrior; one who strives through *jihād*

matn: (n) the text and content of *ḥadīth*

mawḍū': (a) fabricated; an untrue *ḥadīth* which has been fabricated

muhājir (pl: *muhājirūn*)**:** (n) 1). emigrant 2). one who gives up what Allāh ﷻ has prohibited (Bukhārī)

***mursal*:** a *ḥadīth* in which a *tābi'ī* (successor) transmits from Rasūlullāh ﷺ directly

***musnad*:** (n) collection in which Traditions are arranged according to the names of the *Ṣaḥābah*

***muntaqī'*:** a *ḥadīth* going back to the successor only

***mu'ḍal*:** a *ḥadīth* in which two continuous links are missing in one or more places from the *isnād*

***mu'allaq*:** a *ḥadīth* collection which includes Traditions neglected by earlier compilers

***mustakhraj*:** (n) a work in which later scholars revise works of the early major scholars and add to them additional commentaries.

***muttafaqun 'alai-hī*:** (a) agreed upon; any *ḥadīth* which is transmitted by both Bukhārī and Muslim

***mutawātir*:** (a) continuous; a *ḥadīth* reported by a large number of people in different times, to make it impossible for any falsehood to enter it. It is reported by a large number of narrators whose agreement upon a lie is inconceivable. This condition must be met in the entire chain from origin of the report to the end.

***mu'jam*:** (n) a type of collection sometimes arranged according to alphabetical order.

Q

***Qudsī tradition*:** a *ḥadīth* directly inspired by Allāh ﷻ

S

***ṣabr*:** (n) to exercise self-control; will power; control over animal desires; patience; constancy

***ṣadaqah*:** (n) spending voluntarily in the cause of Allāh ﷻ

***ṣadaqah jāriyah*:** (n) recurring charity

***sunnah*:** (n) 1). a practice, a way, a rule, a precedent; a manner of life; 2). traditions and practices of the Prophet ﷺ; used as a complement to the Qur'ān in understanding the laws of Allāh ﷻ

***Ṣaḥābah*:** (n) companions of the Prophet ﷺ

***ṣaḥīḥ*:** (a) the name given to the absolutely correct *ḥadīth* in which there is no weakness and all the transmitters are proven to have possessed both *'adl* and *ḍabt*.

***ṣawm*:** (n) fasting

***sīrah/siyar*:** (n) conduct, deportment, behavior, way of acting

***shahīd*:** (n) martyr

***Ṣuffah*:** (n) the first Islamic University, established in the mosque of the Prophet ﷺ

T

***tafsīr*:** (n) exegesis or explanation into a subject (such as the Qur'ān)

***tābi'ī*:** (n) one who follows; those who succeeded the *Ṣahābah*

U

***'ulamā'*:** (sing: *'ālim*) (n) those learned in Islam

***Ummah*:** (n) the Muslim community

W

***wuḍū'*:** (n) ablution; a special ritual of washing which precedes the Islamic prayers

Z

***zakāh*:** (n) the mandatory giving of alms or charity to the poor; it is calculated as two and a half percent of the one's annual savings; one of the Five Pillars of Islam.